MW01593416

To the Connor Family

God bless!,

Michele Jorgensen

(Gold Star Mother)

FROM
HELL WEEK
TO HEAVEN:

The Life and Times
of
Adam Olin Smith

by

Michele Jorgenson

From Hell Week to Heaven:
The Life and Times of Adam Olin Smith

Copyright © 2011
Michele Jorgenson

The names of some persons have been changed
for their protection and privacy.

All Scripture quotations are taken from
The King James Version of the Holy Bible.

The Scribe's Closet Publications
702 South Missouri
Macon, MO 63552
www.thescribesclosetpublications.com

First Printing, 2011

ISBN 978-0-9832570-2-8

Printed in The United States of America

Acknowledgments

My thanks to God who created us all;
to the A-team: Amber, Audrey, Adam, Andy, Abbie,
Allie, Anna, Austen, and Angel;
to James for his unconditonal love;
and to Susan White for her patience and wisdom.

In loving memory of Adam.

Mom

September 20, 2010-

"For the thing which I greatly feared is come upon me,
And that which I was afraid of is come unto me.
I was not in safety, neither had I rest, neither was I quiet;
Yet trouble came."
---Job 3:25-26

"What in the world is wrong with me?" I cried to myself. It was incredibly late. I was exhausted. Yet, there I lay in bed, wide awake and confused at the emotions building up inside of me. It was as if I were the little "man" atop grandma's old pressure cooker. He would shake violently and whistle shrilly to warn of the rising pressure and possible danger. I tried pulling up my covers, thinking maybe I was cold, then kicking them off in annoyance of the heat.

"I'm not hungry. I'm not thirsty," I reasoned. "Maybe I'm coming down with something. What is it? I could scream out loud."

I finally came to the only "logical" conclusion for my stress. It must be my husband James's fault. I could hear him in the kitchen, banging around in the cupboards, fixing something to eat or drink.

"Did he even once think of me?" I questioned. "Maybe I'm hungry or thirsty. He doesn't even care that I'm upset! He should KNOW that I'm troubled." When I heard the TV come on, I imploded.

"It's journal time!" I hissed. Determinedly, I retrieved the record of my life from under our marriage-bed and let him have it for two whole pages.

For a brief moment, I remembered that this journal was supposed to be different from all the others I had filled for the past twenty-three years. In this one, my great spiritual maturity would be revealed. It would house the record of my righteous prayers and words of wisdom to be passed down to my children and my children's children. Or something like that. But that form of life-literature hadn't lasted long. Soon this notebook about me became like all the others, a mere sounding board when I needed to work out stress.

Finally, my writing hand began to cramp with what my

7

Mother calls Arthur-itis. I slammed the book shut. Later I would destroy those two pages of unfounded anger directed toward the love of my life. Still confused and worried, tears began to flow from me as I turned to the Lord for answers. It would be nice if I could remember to seek God first when I am having a mental melt-down, but I guess that will come along with spiritual maturity. Maybe I can write about it in my next journal.

After a prayer of repentance for my anger, I began to calm down and feel humble. My words to my Heavenly Father turned, as they do nightly, to the status of my nine children. I mentally followed the list from oldest to youngest and, almost routinely, asked for blessings and protection for each one. This particular night, however, seemed different.

When I came to my third child, Adam, my heart began to pound in my chest as I was gripped once again with an escalating sense of dread and helplessness. I told myself that my feelings of fear for him were because of his recent deployment to Afghanistan. Why was I so worried about him? After all, hadn't he and my fourth child, Andy, both served in Iraq at the same time and returned safely? Yet, there was no denying the dread, fear, and thoughts of danger that overcame me in that moment.

Then I prayed to the Lord, words I have recalled and regretted many times since that night. "Father, if you have to call any of my children home to You, please only take the ones that know You and would be "absent from the body and present with You." (2 Corinthians 5:8).

The instant the words left my lips, I tried to call them back. I reasoned with God for several minutes, reminding Him of how much these precious gifts meant to me. I told Him I could withstand any other trial He wanted me to bear, except taking one of my children.

Eventually, I felt that I had made my case clear to God. I asked a special blessing upon Adam, a hedge of protection to surround his life. I drifted off to a fitful sleep.

A few short hours later, in a wicked war-torn country, my baby boy was thrown to his death on a lonely mountain side. His helicopter was ripped in half, expelling all the occupants.

Later, I asked a dear friend of mine, "Did I give God

permission to take my son?"

"Um, God doesn't need permission to take someone," was her wise reply. "He is God."

October 7, 1983-

> "Thou hast covered me in my mother's womb.
> I will praise Thee; for I am fearfully
> and wonderfully made:"
> --Psalm 139: 13-14

"Well, you're still not dilated," droned the too-young, just-filling-in-for-the-day doctor.

I looked over the sheet draped mountain of my nine months pregnant belly and thought, "What does he know anyway?" I wanted to hear him say, "PUSH!" or at least something of that nature.

"Well, let's just stir things up a bit," he announced. All I can say about that is, if you are pregnant and you hear "... let's just stir things up a bit," RUN, (or waddle away), as fast as you can!

Then he sent me home.

This was not my first pregnancy. I had delivered two beautiful little girls, Amber and Audrey, only 10 months apart in 1981. Who does that? Irish twins, I had heard them called, since they were born the same year. Now, only twenty-two months later, I was expecting again.

I had married my sweetheart, Eric, rather quickly the summer before my Senior year of high school. When we were dating, he had mentioned that he did not want to have any children. I should have told him then that I was the most fertile woman on the face of Earth. But who knew? While my classmates prepared to go to Daytona Beach for our Senior trip, I was packing everything we owned into a car and a small U-haul to move to Baton Rouge, Louisiana so my husband could find work.

At home, after the doctor had stirred things up, the pain and cramping continued. I remembered someone saying that if you wanted to go into labor and hurry your delivery, Castor Oil was the answer! I didn't have any Castor Oil in our apartment and I sure wasn't going to drag

9

my two children and big belly over to the neighbors to borrow it. Imagine, a knock at your door and there stands a grotesquely pregnant girl, two toddlers in tow, and a cup in her hand.

"Please Sir, would you happen to have any Castor Oil?"

Somehow I got my greedy little hands on a bottle. The smell of it sickened me, so I decided to dilute it with orange juice. Did you know that oil rises to the top of OJ and floats there in thousands of round, greasy, fish egg bubbles?

I chugged it down. All I can say about that is if you are pregnant and want to speed things up a bit, never drink Castor Oil to do it. I spent most of that day in the bathroom, vomiting and purging. I struggled through the night in turmoil and anxiety, then drifted off into a fitful sleep in the early hours of a new day.

Twenty seven years later, it was de'ja vu.

September 21, 2010-

> "A good name is better than precious ointment;
> And the day of death than the day of one's birth.
> --Ecclesiastes 7:1

I awoke that fateful Tuesday morning, exhausted from the mental turmoil of the night. I regretted losing sleep from worrying for no reason. My husband and I got the three children who still live at home off to school.

Some friends and I had recently opened a pregnancy center. Our goal was to provide a place for women to go for help when faced with an unplanned pregnancy. But we wanted to do more than just hand out supplies. We wanted to share the unconditional love and mercy of the God of the Bible, as well as teaching them about pregnancy, health and parenting skills.

I tried to work on some of the upcoming lessons, yet felt restless and unable to sit still.

"This would be a good time to let people know about Ray of Hope Pregnancy Care Ministries," I thought. There had been no big ad campaign to introduce the ministry. We had concluded at our last board meeting that we needed to go out into the community and share our vision with others who provided services to those in need. With that in mind, I picked up a stack of our business cards to 'campaign for the cause.'

For several hours I kept busy around town, meeting people and talking about the center. I visited a doctor's office, the Sheriff's Department, Police Station, Better Living Center, Victim's Advocate office, spent several minutes at the Literacy Center, and had a nice chat with the Fire Chief before I realized it was almost lunch time.

My last stop was Javasmith, a little coffee place at the south end of town. James, who knows how much I like coffee drinks, had made the mistake of taking me there once. I was hooked!

I ordered my usual, a frappuccino made with skim milk and white chocolate, then dialed the office of the local Middle School.

After twenty years of hit and miss college courses, I had finally earned my Associate Degree. This gave me enough hours to substitute teach. By the time I finally reached my goal, the state legislators had passed a new state law covering substitute teachers. All applications have to be done online. I really struggled with the online application. Then I found out that someone in the Middle School office had gone to an inservice on the application process. I talked to her while I waited for my liquid lunch, and she told me to come in and she would check my application status.

Most of us can look back to when something big happened in our lives and remember exactly where we were or what we were doing. I was driving north on Missouri Street and my cell phone rang. It was my oldest daughter, Amber, who I usually spoke with daily. Carefree, but sleepy, I answered the call that changed my life forever.

Amber was screaming and crying. I thought she was saying "Van, Van, Van!" I immediately feared the worse for her precious little son, Vanderlei, who was only eighteen months old.

"Amber!" I quickly pulled off the road at Lolli's Sale Barn. I spoke loudly to her, using my best mom's-in-charge voice. "You've got to get hold of yourself. Tell me what's wrong."

It worked. She took several deep breaths, and finally blurted out the words, "Mom, some Navy people showed up at Nana and Grandpa Gene's house in Louisiana. They said Adam has been killed in Afghanistan!"

October 8, 1983-

"So God created man in his own image,
In the image of God created he him;"
--Genesis 1:27

"I've been having pains since yesterday," I told Eric as he stood by his dresser preparing to leave for work. "Don't you think you should stay home today?"

"We need the money," was his instant reply. "Besides, you said you're not having REAL contractions."

He had been awakened several times throughout the night with my whining. I kept having pains, but they were so irregular that I thought it was probably false labor.

"I said they can't be real since there is no pattern to them," I agreed, wishing I'd not been so verbal about my uncomfortable condition. "I also said they are getting stronger and are different from my labor with the girls."

This was not how I'd pictured today going. I had seen him in my mind's eye bringing me some toast and juice in bed, plumping up my pillow and offering to rub my aching lower back.

"Baby," he was supposed to say, "I've already called into work and told them I'm not leaving your side today." He had never called me Baby, but I still held out hope.

As he walked out of our bedroom, I was instantly snapped back to reality.

"If you want to keep having these kids," he said carelessly, "somebody has to pay for them."

There he said it! Again, it was about the money! Suddenly I became his judge, jury and executioner.

"OK, well you go to work! I'll stay here alone and have this baby on the floor. Explain that to your friends!" I tried to conjure up some tears to emphasize my hurt, but they wouldn't come. He just shook his head and said goodbye.

I spent the morning with my girls, cleaning up their messes and timing the cramping I was experiencing.

12

Shortly after we had moved to Baton Rouge, two Mormon missionaries had come knocking at our door. They were close enough to our age that we felt as if we could really relate to them. They also seemed to know just what spiritual lifestyle we were seeking for our family. I was the one who first let them into our home. Eric was the one who first said he thought they spoke the truth. Together, we joined the Mormon Church. The congregation welcomed us with open arms and constant fellowship. Now I know this method of gaining members as "love bombing," but that's a whole other book. The decision to join the Mormon church played a major part in the downfall of our marriage, and affected my life decisions for many years.

By ten thirty, I was concerned enough about the strength of my pains to call a woman I knew from the church. I was grateful that she took my two girls home with her, and I called my husband to take me to the hospital. When he finally arrived home, cleaned up and was ready to go, it was lunch-time in down town Baton Rouge.

"Please hurry!" I groaned. My contractions were only eight to ten minutes apart.

Eric seemed to hit every traffic light as it turned red. I just knew we would surely be delivering a baby in our car!

Driving as quickly as the traffic would allow, we arrived at Women's Hospital. I spent the entire day in labor without much progress. At last they wheeled me to the delivery room.

Everyone was dressed in white. Silver gadgets were laid out on tables around the room. The so called bed I was placed upon seemed more like a table. I felt that if I leaned too far in either direction I could fall right off. Didn't I have enough to worry about?

In my excitement to get to the hospital and have this baby (for which I had already chosen a girl's name), I forgot that my regular doctor was out of town. In walked Dr. 'Stir Things Up a Bit.'

"What next?" I wondered. All too soon, I found out.

The baby was huge! I felt as though I had pushed for years. The doctor must have forgotten I was still in the room. He began to talk to the nurses as if I couldn't hear him.

"Wow," he exclaimed in disbelief, "this baby is really

13

stuck!"

That is not what you want to hear when you are exhausted and afraid. I briefly pictured myself walking around for the rest of my life with a child stuck inside of me.

"What did he mean by 'stuck'?" I asked myself. I would have said it out loud but I had more respect for him than he did of me. Besides, I REALLY wanted him to concentrate on exactly what he was doing.

At last the doctor ordered the nurses to hand him the forceps. Even then, he continued to talk about the uniquely lodged-in infant, more to himself than the nurses, as if I did not exist. It would have been comical, if it weren't so frightening.

As the child entered this world, skin as blue as the evening sky, it did not make a sound. The umbilical cord appeared to be wrapped more than once around the baby's neck. The doctor worked for several heart stopping moments before the first cries were heard.

"It's a boy!"

September 21, 2010-

> Yea, though I walk through the valley
> of the shadow of death,
> I will fear no evil: for thou art with me:
> --Psalm 23:4

Amber's words and their meaning shot through my ear canals and crashed into my brain. I felt a part of my spirit die inside of me. For a fraction of a second, time stood absolutely still. Somehow I knew her words were true. Yet I decided to wage war against that truth.

My son, Andy, who was in the Army, had always told me, "Mom, if they call you, we're hurt. If they come to the house, it's worse."

There were times when the boys were both in the war in Iraq when I would picture myself looking out the window of our farm home. I would see the Sheriff's car driving slowly down our road, bearing the worst news a mother could hear.

14

"Amber," I reasoned to both of us, "Think about it. The Navy would not go to tell the grandparents first. That's not the way it's done."

Even as I tried to put Amber's mind at ease, I could see the flaws in my reasoning. I had been married to James for only three years, so my son and I had different last names. The Navy may not have known that. I had also moved several times since Adam had joined, so the Navy may not have had my current address. And, I had been gone from home all day, which meant they could be at my house that very moment!

"Amber, listen," I said in a shaky voice, "don't panic. I'm going to find out what's going on and call you right back."

"Ok, Mom. Bye," she sobbed.

Since I was a little girl, I have known the Lord. I read my Bible. I often felt that I had problems memorizing verses. Yet, they seem to come to me at times in my life when I least expect them. As I pulled out of the sale barn parking lot that day, Romans 8:28 came to mind. "And we know that all things work together for good to them that love God..."

"Lord, you know I love you," I spoke out loud, almost in an angry promise, "but I don't see how any good could EVER come from this!"

Somehow I drove my van north on Missouri Street. I obeyed traffic signals, made a couple turns, and ended up at my husband's chiropractic office, all in a mental daze. I wanted to run to him screaming out my pain. But what if it wasn't true?

I walked quietly through the back door and saw his secretary, Wendy, sitting at her desk. Quickly, I ducked into the bathroom. I remembered just a few weeks before, Wendy and I had stood outside that very office, waving flags as a funeral procession for another fallen soldier had passed. I had been holding a small poster for the boy's mother to see which read, 'Thank you.' When the procession passed, I turned to Wendy and said, "I don't ever want to be in a parade of that kind."

"Dear God," I whispered as I looked into the bathroom mirror, "Don't let it be true! Don't let it be true!"

"I can't stay here," I thought. Slipping out the same

way I came in, I was almost to my van door when I heard my husband's voice.

"Hey, where do you think you are going?" James had heard me leave. "I have something for you. Come back in."

I rounded the front of my van, walking toward him and suddenly felt as if I would pass out. How I yearned for everything to go black, erasing the painful feelings and thoughts. But I stayed conscious.

I stopped and bent down, putting my hands on my knees. James was instantly concerned. "What's wrong, Sweety?" he asked like a chiropractor, "Does your back hurt?" He came down the stairs to me and I threw my arms around his neck.

"Amber called and said Adam's been killed in Afghanistan," I numbly spoke the words.

My sensitive, loving husband burst into tears. "No, not Adam, not Adam," he sobbed.

We held each other for several minutes. "I need my children," I told him. He helped me into his car, then stepped inside to tell Wendy to cancel his appointments for the rest of the day. We drove to the school.

On our way Amber called again. "Mom, there are some Navy guys at Dad's house now."

For twenty-nine years I have been the protector of my children. I've dealt with toddlers, teachers, law enforcement, abusive boyfriends, illnesses, broken bones, teenagers, hurt feelings, and more. But there was nothing I could do to stop this terror-train from barreling down on my family.

"Where was I when my Adam needed me the most?" I thought. "I'm on the other side of the world." My mind went numb. I could barely function.

"Amber, where are you at right now?" I asked, trying to distract her.

"I'm in St. Louis at one of my stores." She replied. Amber worked for a company that stocked CDs and DVDs in department stores. She was good at her job and just about everything else she did. I was very proud of her career. I became even more proud of her when she decided to stay home and become a full time mom. She was supposed to work only a few more days in St. Louis, then

16

move to Columbia with her husband, Brad, and little Van.

"Can you get to Columbia?" I asked.

"Yes, Brad's mom is coming to get me. I can't drive," was her weak reply.

"Where is Andy?" I asked her. Andy had been staying at Eric's since his return from Iraq. Instead of re-enlisting, he had joined the National Guard and was attending college.

"He is at Dad's," she informed me.

My already broken heart ached even more when I thought of my son, Andy. He was born only twenty months after Adam. His entire life was spent as Adam's best friend.

"We have to tell the other children. I will call you back soon."

We stopped at the Middle School. Stepping through those doors, I thought how different this was from what I had planned. Only minutes before, I was to speak to someone about substitute teaching. How would we tell the children? Now I was, forever, a changed person.

James spoke to the secretary who paged my two youngest to come to the office. Austen, age thirteen and Angel, age eleven were brought at the same time. They searched our pale, grieving faces for answers but I could not speak. My husband told them. We stood in a huddle of tears for several minutes.

I eventually whispered, "We have to tell Anna." We walked slowly to James' car and drove to the High School. We went through the same routine of telling the office staff. Someone went to retrieve my seventh child, Anna.

When she came into view she instantly knew we bore bad news. She began to cry, "What happened? What happened?" My husband just said, "Adam" and Anna's knees buckled. She collapsed to the floor. Again I wished for sweet darkness to overtake me so I wouldn't have to witness the pain of my children. I didn't want to know the truth. But I remained awake, and we ushered the sad group to the car.

As my husband drove, I called Audrey. She was crying. "Amber called me about Adam."

"Do you want to come home?"

"Jessye is on his way to get me from work." She and Jessye had been married for over seven years and had four beautiful children.

Briefly, I pictured Audrey as a little girl when Adam was born. She had been a thumb sucker. When she was very tired, she needed her thumb in her mouth. Adam was like her security blanket. Her free hand wanted to be rubbing his bald little head.

"Don't go there!" I warned my mind. "Keep it together for the kids."

Next, we stopped by the service station where my daughter Abbie worked. She was only a few months from having her first baby. I feared for her health with such tragic news.

"Abbie, we've lost Adam in Afghanistan," I cried. She came from behind the counter and hugged me. Shaking and crying, she left with us immediately.

There was only one more child to break the news to in Macon, my daughter Allie. By then we needed more room in our vehicle, so I suggested we retrieve my van.

When we entered Allie's apartment en mass, she jokingly said, "Wow, to what do I owe this visit from everyone?" I knelt on the floor by her chair and told her the news. We gathered her and adorable little son, Jericho, and headed home.

As we approached our little farm near Ten Mile my heart began to pound. I was sure the Navy personnel would be sitting in my drive, waiting for me like they were at Eric's house. But when we turned in, no one was there.

"Maybe everyone was wrong after all!" I wondered hopefully.

In this age of technology, I had not even exited my van before I was bombarded with sympathy calls. I asked one of Adam's high school friends how he had heard about my son. He said someone read about it on the internet. Later I looked up the first messages to me and realized that everyone online knew about my son's death before Amber's first call to me! I removed my name and page from this source of information. I felt so exposed.

People who had never stepped foot into my home suddenly showed up. An hour after I returned home, with a house full of people, the official Navy grief-bearers finally arrived.

Two uniformed men were led into my living room where I sat. They stood solemnly and said, "Mrs. Jorgenson, we

18

have come to inform you that your son, SO2 Adam Olin Smith, was killed early this morning in a Black Hawk helicopter crash in the Province of Zabul, Afghanistan.

"Was he shot down?"

"We don't know."

"Would you tell me if you did know?"

They couldn't even say that much. I became a bit obsessed with the thought of my brave boy being shot down and falling from the sky.

Then Amber called.

"Dad and I are being driven to the St. Louis airport. The Navy is flying us to Dover, Delaware to meet the plane. Adam is coming home. If you can get to the airport in less than three hours, you can go along."

Something about it didn't seem right, but I had no time to argue.

"Get me a ticket. I'll be there."

I had two thoughts on that drive. One, I wanted someone to pay for killing my son. And two, I just wanted to bring him home. The military had kept him long enough.

October 8, 1983-

For this child I prayed;
And the Lord hath given me my petition
which I asked of him:
--1 Samuel 1:27

"I have a son?" I asked the hospital staff for the third time.

"Do you want to be the one to tell your husband?" inquired the doctor.

"He's not such a bad doctor," I thought. "After all, everything turned out alright."

As they wheeled me out of the delivery room I saw Eric standing in the doorway.

"It's a boy!" I told him, lifting my head weakly from the cot.

I will never forget the expression of disbelief on his face at that moment. "It's a BOY?" You would have thought we had twelve daughters and had been trying for a son for ten years the way we acted. Yet, for some reason neither of us had expected a boy.

I could not fall asleep, but not from pain or discomfort. I could not close my eyes because I could not stop staring into the tiny face of my first-born son. What a miracle! Our bonding was immediate.

By the next day we still had not chosen a name for the baby. Nothing seemed to fit well with our daughters' names, Amber and Audrey. Once, when I obviously had too much time on my hands, I read an article stating that if parents start a pattern in their children's names they must continue with it or the child left out could need counseling for the rest of his life. Or something like that.

"If you don't have a name picked out before you leave the hospital," one word-wielding, power tripping nurse informed us "we have to write John Doe on his birth certificate." The thought terrified my twenty year old mind.

That night, after Eric had left to go home, I lay in my hospital bed, propped up on pillows with my baby son snuggled close to me. I turned on the television and flipped through the channels. A movie was just starting that held my attention. It was the story of Adam Walsh, a young boy who had been kidnapped and murdered. My heart broke at the thought of losing a child. When the movie ended, I decided then and there to name my son after this unfortunate little boy. I imagined my Adam growing up and living a full life in honor of that little Adam.

The following day Eric agreed with my choice of names.

"But what about a middle name?" he asked as he sat at the end of my bed. So far each of our children's middle names were after a family member.

That day Eric's Grandpa Blackorby from Missouri had come to visit.

"Grandpa, what is your middle name?" Eric asked.

"Olin," he replied.

"Adam Olin!" Eric and I said it together. We both smiled.

"Grandpa, what would you think if we named our baby Adam Olin, after you?" asked Eric.

Grandpa beamed and said, "That'd be all right."

By the next day I was ready to go home but Adam wasn't. He had developed a case of yellow jaundice. I had

experienced this before with Amber, so I wasn't worried.
I had taken her home to lay in front of a sunny window.
These doctors disagreed with that treatment. They wanted
him to stay one more night in the hospital, under their
special lights for yellow jaundice.

I understood, but there was no room for me to stay
another night. Another woman needed my room, so I was
being kicked out. I did not argue. But as I packed up my
few belongings, I began to realize I would be leaving there
without my son. The tears began.

"I can't leave him here!" I tried to explain to everyone
who would listen. No one seemed to understand.

"It's just one night" consoled a kind nurse.

Even Eric missed my empty-arms anxiety. "Hey,
someone from work gave us two tickets to an LSU football
game tonight! That will take your mind off of things." He
went to get the car.

As the nurse slowly pushed me out to the car in a wheel
chair, I could not hold back the tears and began sobbing. I
was sure that anyone who saw me must have thought I'd
lost my baby or something.

At home, I cried all afternoon.

We had great seats at the football game that night. By
then I was in control of my water works, yet very sad. I
watched three little boys play nearby. They must have been
about six or seven years old. One had curly blond hair and
blue eyes. His beautiful smile made him stand out from all
the rest.

I thought of my new born son and wondered what type
boy he would turn out to be. Of course my heart went out
to my new baby. He was being bottle fed that night and was
probably yearning for his mommy.

When we finally arrived home, I walked into our
bedroom and up to the empty crib. This was not what I had
planned for my first night home. Once again I could not
help crying.

"We're going after him in the morning," was Eric's
supposed-to-be-consoling remark. "We should enjoy a good
night's sleep while we can."

"You don't understand," I sobbed, "I want my son!"

September 21, 2010-

> Be ye angry, and sin not:
> Let not the sun go down upon your wrath:
> --Ephesians 4:26

"We'd better be bombing someone soon!" I said out loud as I drove like a mad woman to St. Louis. "Something will be done to retaliate even if I have to push the button myself!"

My mind couldn't stop imagining my boy falling helplessly from the sky. Was he afraid? Did he have time to know what was happening? Did he suffer! Worse yet, had he survived and been tortured?

"Don't go there! Don't go there!" I pleaded with myself. "Concentrate on the task at hand."

My time frame for catching the flight to Dover was quickly passing. It seemed like I had a million exits to pass before reaching the one for the airport.

Amber called my cell phone. "Mom, where are you now?" she asked frantically. "We're all checked in and everything!"

I wanted to be annoyed at someone for not driving THE MOTHER to the airport and getting HER 'all checked in and everything'. But I didn't even know where to aim my wrath. And, I realized, it wouldn't do anyone any good to complain now. My son was gone, and no one could change that.

"But whoever caused his death can still pay for it in blood!" I fell back into revenge mode until I reached the parking garage of the airport.

As I ran up to the door I saw Amber waiting for me. Standing next to her was an officer from the Navy SEALs.

"Mom, this is Matt." Amber introduced us. "Matt, this is my Mom."

"Nice to meet you, Ma'am." He stated formally shaking my hand. "I'm so sorry for your loss."

"Thank you," I felt weak at the sight of his Navy uniform.

As I looked around the airport, a wave of grief engulfed me. How many times had I met my Adam here? Wasn't it just a year ago when he came walking around that corner

22

looking like an officer in his uniform? Part of me wanted to let loose and run screaming through the building at the injustice of it all. Quietly, I picked up my carry-on and followed Matt to the waiting plane.

The passengers were unusually quiet as we entered. Our last-minute seats were at the very back of the plane. Once we were seated, the pilot made an announcement about some poor family of a fallen soldier being on board. Everyone began to clap. I snapped out of my thoughts for a moment to realize he meant us. I began to cry.

"I'm sorry for your loss." I heard a voice above my head. It was a male flight attendant, looking down at me. Again, those heart-felt words were spoken to me. I would grow accustomed to the meaning of them as I heard them again and again.

Moments later everyone was buckled in and we were taking off. The engines began to roar and we began to move. Panic engulfed me. What were the last sounds my son heard? Were they as loud as the engines I was hearing?

"What really happened?" I screamed inside my head as I looked out my window into the darkness.

I finally allowed my thoughts to turn to my God. I had been avoiding Him for hours.

"Why'd You do that? Why'd You do that?" I whispered over and over.

It was not that I believed He had killed my son. Rather, I felt that He could have protected him and hadn't. I was so hurt! I have turned my back on Him many times in my life, then repented and returned to Him. But that day was the only time I felt that God had turned His back on me.

I recalled the time that King David found out that his son, Absalom, a mighty warrior, had been killed. "O my son Ab'-sa-lom, my son, my son Ab'-sa-lom! Would God I had died for thee, O Ab'-sa-lom, my son, my son!" David cried. (2 Samuel 18:33)

"Father, why didn't you take me instead!" I whispered, sobbing. "I've lived a full life. Adam's was just beginning!"

"Excuse me," a young female flight attendant interrupted my mourning. "We have seats for your family up front if you like." I didn't care to move, but didn't want to appear ungrateful. As we moved forward to the front of the plane, I felt as if all the passengers were staring at us.

I don't think the stewardess ever told us her name, but her memory will stay with us forever. She checked on us constantly, offering food, drinks and pillows. None of which we wanted, but we were still grateful for her sincere care.

"Do you mind if I share with you for a moment?" She asked as she knelt on the floor at my knee. I wondered what one so young could possibly say to console my anguish.

"That's fine." I agreed to listen to her.

"Well," she began, "I just wanted to tell you that I lost my son a few weeks ago, too."

"What?" I replied in disbelief. "I'm so sorry." It was all I could think to say.

She told Amber and I that she had lost her precious baby boy at only sixteen months. She handed me a small glass heart that someone had given to her when her baby died. She wanted me to have it. I was moved to tears. A few weeks later, I attended a funeral for another young man. I sent his mother the tiny glass heart to symbolize our shared grief.

A short time later we landed at O'Hare airport in Chicago. We had missed our connecting flight and there wasn't another until morning. Of course, our luggage wouldn't be released to us until we arrived in Dover, Delaware. We spent the night at a motel near the airport. After hours of crying, I fell asleep and instantly dreamed of Adam.

In the dream I was standing in front of a huge picture of a wooded area surrounding a large lake. My Adam was swimming right in the middle of the lake! As I sadly stared at the picture, it suddenly came to life. His muscular arms cut through the water as he always had. Also there were a few of his friends swimming with him. He swam to the shore and climbed out. Everyone in the picture but Adam knew he would soon die. When they all climbed out of the water, they were acting unusually quiet compared to his laughing and joking spirit. They gave each other knowing looks, warning themselves not to tell him.

Finally he said, "What's going on you guys?" No one would say. I awoke with a start and began to cry loudly. That was the only dream I've had of my son since his death.

My wailing woke Amber up. "Mom, are you ok?" She inquired.

"No," I sobbed, "I want my son!"

October 18, 1983-

> As arrows are in the hand of a mighty man;
> so are children of the youth.
> Happy is the man that hath his quiver full of them:
> --Psalm 127: 4-5

"Eric," I called from our bedroom, "were you holding Adam just a few minutes ago?" Baby Adam had been home from the hospital for a week. We had settled into a nice family routine with him.

"I'm watching a game in here. What do you need?" was Eric's not-really-wanting-to-know reply from the comfort of his favorite chair in the living room.

"I don't NEED anything," I mumbled, more to myself than to him. I knew that interrupting his sports on TV would really annoy him. But curiosity and confusion won and I persisted.

"I know I laid Adam on his back before I left the room a while ago." I said as I walked into the sports arena and interrupted a good play. "That's the third time today I've gone back into the room and he has been lying in a different position!"

"Well, he's rolling over now," was Eric's wise reply as he tried to look around me to see the TV.

"You don't understand," I simplified for him, "Babies do not roll over at a week and a half, especially from their backs to their tummies!"

"OK, he's special." That was the last communication that I received for at least an hour.

"Babies can't roll over this young, can they?" I wondered to myself as I entered the girls' room to watch them play. "When did Amber roll over for the first time?"

Sitting on Amber's Strawberry Shortcake covered bed my thoughts were drawn back to her birth. It had been a frightening experience. I had twelve hours of labor, then had to push so hard that I broke blood vessels all over my face. I looked as if I had the chicken pox. I hadn't been offered any pain medicine, and didn't know to ask for it. The pressure of straining so hard left its mark temporarily.

Good old Doctor Campbell delivered Amber. Later he told Eric about me, "She's a keeper." Maybe Eric thought he was talking about the baby.

I was still trying to finish high school when we brought Amber home. Eric's parents had allowed us to move into their basement. I didn't really bond with my baby at first. I would kiss her goodbye and hand her over to my mother-in-law, Lucille, in the mornings. Then I didn't see her again until the bus dropped me off in the evenings.

Amber seemed to cry all the time with me at first. I worked hard to get her to sleep so that I could do my homework. Yet, every time I lay her down, she would wake up!

"She just wants to see your face," Lucille told me one day when Amber was two months old. I had been struggling with her for an hour in our daily battle, trying to study.

Lucille was exactly right, I discovered. When I placed Amber in a pumpkin seat in the center of the table, she became as quiet as a church mouse and watched me!

"How strange," I thought. "She really likes me after all." I felt guilty for not knowing what my baby wanted. Before long I was making funny faces at her and forgetting the all-important homework.

After we moved to Baton Rouge, Amber and I bonded completely. I wouldn't let anyone else around her.

"Even then," I remembered, "at two months old she wasn't rolling over. What about Audrey?"

I tried to remember my second child's infancy. There were far less trials with her than with Amber. This was partly due to the fact that I had gone through everything just ten months before. And partly because she has a whole different personality. Where Amber tended to be a bit demanding, Audrey was a happy and contented baby girl.

"No, even though Audrey was different than Amber in many ways," I recalled, "she too did not roll over until she was about two months old!"

I slipped back into my bedroom once again to check on Adam. There he lay, sleeping soundly just like I had left him.

"I see what you are doing," I whispered to him. "You know I'm on to your little tricks don't you. What a clever little man you are! OK, now I'm talking to a newborn as if he understands me. The next thing you know I will be blaming him for rearranging items whenever I can't find something in the house!"

September 22, 2010-

> For now we see through a glass, darkly;
> But then face to face:
> now I know in part;
> but then shall I know even as also I am known.
> --1 Corinthians 13:12

"Could I have been a better Mom for Adam?" I lay there in the dark, in a hotel room in Chicago, and began to drag up old wounds and memories. "Of course I could have! What Mom doesn't feel she could have done better?"

My mind wandered back to Adam's Senior year in high school. I was driving him to a ball game in Atlanta, and for some reason he was mad at me.

"You're a bad parent," he informed me.

It did not hurt as much as other statements he had made to me in the past. I knew he loved me and he knew I loved him, so I pursued the subject.

"Ok, Bud, tell me exactly how I've been a bad parent and maybe I can work on it."

"I don't know, you're just a bad parent."

"Well, I'm sure sorry about that," was my reply. Then I said the words I've said several times to my teenagers when they have pointed out my flaws as a mother. "When you have children and raise them perfectly then you can come back and tell me I'm a bad parent."

I continued to pretend to be in charge and secure. But I didn't let it go. Inside my head I plunged into my usual guilt trip--all the harm I had caused my babies.

"Poor children, they didn't stand a chance with me as their mother!" I kept driving.

Remembering that conversation didn't help. "I'm the

worst mom ever! Adam was right," I thought with an aching heart.

"Enough of this!" I jumped out of bed to dress for the next flight. Today I would bring my son home, or so I thought.

Matt proved to be a God-send. We went about multiple airports in a daze and he kept us all together. I could see him whisper a few times to different flight attendants and gate workers. They would then look at us with sympathy and rush us past the lines of passengers. I didn't have the strength to say, "Don't look at me like that!"

Before I realized it, I found myself in Dover, Delaware. We were taken to a beautiful hotel for the night, where our luggage had already arrived. We could shower and finally change our clothes.

There were a total of nine dead from Adam's fateful flight. Four were Navy SEALs. The others were a mix of Army, Navy, and civilians. The families of the fallen SEALs were all at this same hotel to greet their loved ones. There were groups of people huddled together in various places, crying. There were individuals standing around as if numbness had overtaken their senses.

Matt explained to us that in a short while we would be taken to a military base. What he was saying finally penetrated my numbness.

"Adam will be flown into this base shortly." He said.

"Mom," Amber found me in the foyer of the hotel. "Some of Adam's friends are here. They drove up from Virginia Beach. I don't think they were supposed to do that, but they are in Dad's room right now." I quickly followed her to the elevator.

As we entered Eric's room I saw four tired, sad young sailors standing on the other side of the bed. I wanted to run to them all and hug them but I didn't. I walked in shyly and was introduced to each of them.

The first to step forward was Little Wally. He was the spitting image of my own father, Keith, in his Navy uniform! I couldn't help but stare. I learned that he was Adam's best friend in Virginia. His eyes were sorrowful and sunken from lack of sleep and the pain of what had just happened.

The next boy I noticed was Jason. He reminded me of

one of Adam's friends from Missouri named Clark. He was quiet and had a shy smile.

Then I was introduced to Ricky. He had a thin mustache, which surprised me. I thought they had to be clean shaven.

The last SEAL we met was Luke. He too did not speak much.

Eric made some small talk about the boys leaving without permission, but I couldn't keep silent any longer.

"What happened?"

Ricky looked surprised, "You don't know?"

I shook my head.

"It was a brown out." When I looked confused, he explained. "When a chopper kicks up a lot of dust, it can cause the visibility to almost disappear."

"You mean they were close to the ground?" I felt as if the air had been knocked from me. This was my first clue that my son did not fall from the sky as I had envisioned. Could he have been just a few feet from the ground? Why couldn't they have jumped out? It was a week before I got all the details of the story.

Matt came to the door. "They're ready to go," he announced.

We were loaded onto three small buses. The drive to the base seemed short. Once there, we were escorted into a building that was designed just to greet the families of fallen soldiers. The room we were taken to was elegantly decorated with floral printed furniture, rich dark colored coffee tables and flowers. I felt as if I were about to enter a banquet.

The four families dispersed into groups in the various sections of living rooms. Several military people walked around and asked us if we would care for a drink or snack. Four chaplains were introduced to us. Each went to sit with a different family.

A black male chaplain introduced himself and sat down next to me. "How are you doing?" he questioned.

"Not too good," was the only answer I could say.

"I can pray with you if you like," he offered. I accepted. He asked God for peace and comfort and all the other emotional needs we lacked. I felt nothing. Then the chaplain asked me what else he could do for us.

"Well," I said. "There are four of my son's friends who

drove all night to meet Adam. I'm not sure where they are now. I haven't seen them since the hotel. Can you say a prayer with them?"

"I won't be able to do that. But I can send a message for another chaplain to pray with them."

I didn't understand. Was this man assigned exclusively to my family? Were there formalities that kept him from ministering to the boys? Are they in trouble for coming here without permission? The questions remained in my head. Somehow I knew that these people had gone through this type of comforting session before.

"Could everyone please turn and face the Admiral?" a young sailor announced from the front of the room. In walked an older gentleman in a light brown uniform. He was flanked by several other sailors. He walked across the room and stopped right behind the couch I was sitting on. I'm not sure why I felt so honored to see him. Maybe it was the air of authority he carried with him. Maybe it was the way everyone in military uniform seemed to straighten up taller.

The Admiral was introduced and he began to speak. "People, I'm an old fart…" Then his voice cracked and he teared-up. "But this doesn't ever get any easier." He tried several times to regain his composure. Everyone was holding their breath.

I remembered that there were boxes of tissues scattered about the room. One was sitting on the table right in front of me. The mom in me took over and, without thought or care of protocol, I grabbed a box and held it out to him. There was a quick intake of breath from the military personnel in the room.

"It's too late now to take it back," I thought.

The Admiral just smiled and stepped forward and accepted a couple tissues. I placed the box back on the table. He could not speak again and turned and strode out of the room with his group. I realized then that he felt responsible for every soldier who served under him. I was humbled that he cared for my son even if he had not known him personally.

We were informed that the plane had arrived that carried our sons. We were told what order they would be carried off the plane. My Adam was to be third.

Then we were instructed to place our right hands on our hearts as each boy was removed and carried to a waiting van. Once again we were led to the buses and driven across the air field to the plane.

The time had come to witness the final return of my first born son from the war. My heart pounded as we covered the short distance to the field. "What will I do?" I wondered. "How will I act?"

Again I wondered where Adam's friends had gone. Weren't they allowed to be there after all?

Before I had time to gather my thoughts and emotions, the first coffin was being carried from the back of the plane. The mother standing to my left whimpered weakly and fainted. Her family responded quickly by lifting her into a chair and caring for her needs.

The second mother began to moan loudly as her son was carried from the plane to the van. My heart went out to those mothers. They had endured this sight as best they could.

I was next. I wasn't sure how I would react to the sight of my son's coffin.

"God help me! I can't stand here! I can't watch this!" I prayed.

Suddenly, it was my turn. A long silver casket draped with a flag emerged from the plane.

A sense of incredible pride welled up inside of me. I stood a little taller and slowly lifted my hand to my heart. What a brave son I had! He actually gave up his life for our country. Although my tears flowed freely, I maintained my composure.

"Thank you, God," I whispered. I watched as the fourth boy was carried out.

I learned later that Adam's friends were there after all. They had stood at attention around his casket until the plane was empty. What an honor.

My Adam was home from the war.

August 29, 1987-

> For Thou art my hope, O Lord God:
> Thou art my trust from my youth.
> --Psalm 71:5

A while ago Adam came up to me, (I'm talking about a three year old boy!), and said, "You know, Mommy, you can't change the world."

Surprised at such a comment, I asked, "Do you want to change the world?"

"Yes."

"Well then, how can we do it?" He put his hand to his face and pinched his bottom lip together with his fingers. He had a habit of doing this when he was deep in thought.

"We could scrape all the paint off our house and paint it a different color!" His world is pretty small right now.

I've begun to notice that there is something very different about this child from my other children. It's not that he is demanding in a selfish way or anything. But there is an air of authority which everyone seems to respect, including me.

By now I had convinced Eric to move us all back to our home town in Missouri. He loved Baton Rouge and had moved home only because of my desire to return. He bought us a lovely house near the ball park, with a wonderful big yard and huge old trees everywhere.

The children and I spent many happy hours together. Long walks through fields and woods became a special treat. We loved breathing in nature. This helped us to break the monotony of being in the house.

Just a few minutes into a walk, I would usually hear from Adam, "Carry me." He never really cried or whined to get his way. He would simply make a statement and expect me to cater to him.

"Andy is walking," I would inform him. "And he is younger than you!" Andy, my fourth child was very quiet and loving. He lived for the outdoors and never seemed to mind his older brother being carried instead of him.

"Carry me."

Adam's repeated request was followed with a refusal to walk another step. As always, I would walk back to him and hoist him up. There would be no cuddling though. He would ride like royalty upon my hip with his back as straight as a board.

To help pay the bills so that I was able to stay home with my children, I began to babysit during the week. At times I would have up to eight extra little voices demanding to be heard. Adam did not lack for playmates.

The local Baptist minister and his wife had two sons almost the same ages as my Adam and Andy. So sometimes I babysat for them. Soon Adam had a best buddy in their older son, Obie. They were best friends for Adam's entire life.

Our house became a hangout for many of the neighborhood children, too. It wasn't uncommon for a group of us to be sitting in the grass somewhere in our yard. They would listen intently as I spun some made-up story to entertain them. Our days were filled with laughter and sunshine.

"Mommy, what's a 'vorce.' Adam inquired of me one day as we lay on our backs in the grass. We had been picking out different shapes from the white fluffy clouds that dotted the sky.

I realized that he had overheard Eric and I talking the night before about some disturbing news we had heard. Our friends had married only a month before our wedding. We had spent many good times with them playing cards and going out to movies. But recently, they had decided to end their marriage.

"It's called a divorce, Buddy. It's when two people who are married decide to break up and live in different houses." As the reality of what I'd just told him sunk in, I saw a look of great concern cross Adam's face.

"You don't have to worry about YOUR Mommy and Daddy though," I reassured him. "That will NEVER happen to us."

As the words passed my lips, the sun chose that moment to hide behind a huge fluffy cloud. A chilly breeze swirled through the air raising goose bumps on my arms.

Dark and confusing days were at our own door.

September 22, 2010-

> For I know the thoughts that I think toward you,
> saith the Lord,
> Thoughts of peace, and not of evil,
> To give you an expected end.
> --Jeremiah 29:11

We stood at the airfield, watching the truck that received our fallen sons until it turned out of sight. All the families were silent on our trip back to the hotel. Upon returning to our rooms, we rested and pondered what had just taken place.

I had expected to go home with Adam's body. But I was told that an autopsy would have to be performed before he could be taken home.

At some point Adam's girlfriend, Charlotte arrived. She was so very sad and, like me, she was just going through the motions of communicating with the people around her. We visited for a short while in a living room of the hotel until Matt came up to us.

"We need to meet with the coroner in just a little bit," he said sadly.

I didn't understand why but agreed to go. Charlotte and T-Roy, a good friend to Adam's who had driven Charlotte the four hours from Virginia Beach, went with me. We entered a conference room where Eric and the coroner, dressed in blue camouflage, sat waiting.

"Mrs. Jorgenson, there are a few details we need to discuss and papers for you to sign," the man in blue said gently. I realized with horror just what this meeting was all about.

"We will be opening the casket within a day or two. At this time, we don't know the condition of your son's body. Among the possibilities are charred remains or just body parts…"

My stomach turned. I must have turned white with shock.

"Wait a minute!" T-Roy interjected. "I don't see any reason Adam's mother should be hearing this."

I was impressed that one so young discerned my anguish before the other, more seasoned men in the room. Eric and the coroner agreed that it would be best for me to wait outside. Although I did not like the fact that Eric would be making decisions about my son without me, I felt light headed and faint. Charlotte accompanied me into the hall right outside the door.

We spoke about Adam for a few minutes. Then the door opened and the men came out. The coroner apologized for upsetting me.

"I understand why you have to do this. But what you were saying was really messing with my mental picture. I have been imagining my son looking like he's asleep," I explained.

I was completely drained by then, and was developing a headache. I told the others I needed to lie down. Eric went out to dinner with the group. He needed to eat as he had only consumed alcohol for the past twenty-four hours.

I felt bad for not spending more time with Charlotte, but I wanted to lie down. Amber decided to go back to our room with me. She was reserved and quiet, needing time to cry like I did.

Without warning, unwanted thoughts would spring into my mind. Once in bed, the thought came to me suddenly, "I will not see, or speak to, or hug my Adam again, for as long as I live. I shouldn't be eating or drinking or even breathing right now since he can no longer do those things!"

The next day we were flying back to Missouri. During one of our layovers we sat as a group at the airport. Matt was kneeling in front of me, explaining some procedures that were to take place in the near future, when he received a call.

I could tell from the tone and expression on his face it was someone in authority who had surprising news. We anxiously waited for his call to end.

"Wow," he began. "That's interesting. That was the coroner. He said they had opened Adam's casket and there he was. They knew him instantly. They did not need any dental records or identification to recognize him."

I knew a miracle had taken place. God's first gift to me had arrived. I imagined that Adam had just bumped his head and gone to sleep. Could that have been what actually happened? There in the crowded airport we wept openly.

We landed in the St. Louis airport around midnight. Matt was driving Eric and Amber back to Columbia. I would be driving myself home.

I was in constant contact with my husband until the last thirty miles. He was concerned about me driving, but I reminded him that for the last sixteen years I had been driving ambulances in inclement weather, and under stress and fatigue. That seemed to console him.

After he hung up for the last time, I found myself alone

with my thoughts. I could not stand the noise of the radio. In the silence I began to softly tell God how hurt I was. I realized that He already knew this. That thought made me furious.

"Why? Why? Why?" I began to scream, forgetting the miracle at the airport. "My baby, my baby, You took my baby!"

The more I stressed these facts to my Maker, the louder I screamed. I screamed so loud and so long that I had to quickly pull off the road. Throwing myself across the passenger seat, I shoved open the door, and vomited.

Spent, I lay there for quite some time. I could hear cars driving by and feel the cool night wind blowing across my face.

I looked up into a dark silent field of harvested corn and once more asked quietly, "Why God?"

No answer came.

July 6, 1987-

> And unto the married I command,
> yet not I, but the Lord,
> Let not the wife depart from her husband:
> --I Corinthians 7:10

"Hey Eric, you wanna beer?" One of Eric's slow-pitch softball team mates called out to him. Laughter floated through the air. Several ball players crowded around a pickup truck. They were drinking as they did every Sunday before a game.

I had stopped by the ball park to tell him I was headed to another church meeting. As he leaned into my car window, he heard the jeering remark. He couldn't hide his disappointment in me. There I was, all dressed up for church with my children strapped into the back seat. The other men's wives sat around the ball field, some in bikini tops, soaking up the sun. Their children were playing happily in the grass nearby.

"I have no choice," I thought helplessly. "I have to go back the thirty miles to church and help. I have several callings! How can I say I can't make it?"

36

I was a teacher for young women, a visiting teacher for three other mothers, a basketball coach for a church team and part of a presidency for the entire young women's organization. The more responsibility I accepted with the church, the farther Eric and I moved from each other emotionally.

And there was the "encouragement" of our separate groups of friends. My friends were all members of the Mormon Church. I had either ignored my worldly friends or they were avoiding me in fear that I was trying to convert them. I was officially a religious fanatic.

"Michele, Eric doesn't deserve you." My closest friend would tell me. "You deserve so much better. He doesn't even care that you and your kids need to be sealed to a priesthood holder to get to the Celestial Kingdom." That last comment always drove home the realization that my husband did not love us enough to take us to heaven!

His friends were all former classmates and ball players that he had run with for years. They had one or two children at the most. We had four babies in five years! Our pictures of a happy family were quite different from theirs.

"I'm getting sick and tired of you acting like you're so much better than everyone else!" Eric's words stung me later that night when I finally arrived home. It seemed that at some point in every argument, these words were thrown at me.

"What's happening to us?" I cried to myself. "Why does he hate me so?" We were under a lot of pressure. Who wouldn't buckle? I went to bathe the children and put them to bed.

"Mommy, sing to us," Adam requested his usual nightly routine. It didn't matter how many songs I sang or stories I told, he would always want 'just one more.' I used to think it was because of my beautiful voice, but later I realized he had a fear of being left in the dark. He wanted me there until he fell asleep. Whatever the reason, I did not mind. I enjoyed those last wakeful minutes at night with my children.

I would recall songs I had sung in school and church as a child and sing them to my babies. They soon became my children's favorites: One Tin Soldier, Where Have All the Flowers Gone, Because He Lives, and more. Adam liked

You Are My Sunshine. When I sang it, he would wait until I said "sunshine" each time and, in his sweet little voice, he would sing "sunshine."

This particular night, before Adam dozed off to sleep, he asked, "Is Daddy mad at you?"

"He is just tired, Buddy," I assured him. "Go to sleep."

"I will if you sing some more."

"Ok, but this is the very last song," I smiled and began to sing.

September 24, 2010-

> Rejoice with them that do rejoice,
> And weep with them that weep.
> --Romans 12:15

"Mom, people have been stopping by our house since you left." I awoke to Anna telling me the refrigerator and freezer were full of food. Casseroles, side dishes, desserts--the list was endless. Our neighbors and friends wanted to express their sympathy. We appreciated it so much. I couldn't have cooked a meal anyway. I wanted to curl up in a fetal position and remain in bed for the rest of my life. But my family needed me. And I had a funeral to plan.

A mother never expects to bury her son. It's supposed to be the other way around. Once I saw a movie where one mother said, "It's against Nature," as her son was put into the ground. Whatever that means, it just did not seem right. The next five days were a blur of preparations.

At one point, Eric, James and I were sitting at the funeral home, discussing the arrangements with Kyle, the funeral director. Eric said, "I don't care what you do. I just don't want any sad songs."

"Doesn't he realize that, at a funeral, any song will be a sad song?" I thought to myself.

I was surprised to learn that Adam liked George Strait's music. When he left for the Navy, you couldn't have paid him to listen to country music. We determined that a George Strait song would be sung at his funeral. Not much progress but at least a step forward.

A few days later I received a call from Kyle. "Michele,

we may have a problem." He sounded concerned. "I don't believe our funeral home is large enough to hold all those who will want to come and pay their respects to Adam."

Nothing fazed me now. I had already experienced the worse thing in the world. Anything beyond Adam's death was just a minor setback. "Ok, maybe we can use the school."

"Yes, or the National Guard armory," he suggested. It took only a moment for us to come to our real choice. My family and I attended the First Baptist Church. "Do you think they will allow us to have the funeral there?" Kyle asked.

"I'm sure they will, but I will call Pastor John right now." They were honored to help us. After that, everything seemed to fall into place for my son's final ceremony.

I immediately thought of two people who sing like Angels. They both attended my church. Matt Carroll had a voice like the best country singer, and he loved George Strait! And, Jamee Bowen often blessed our congregation with powerful songs of praise and worship. They both said yes. Matt would search for an appropriate George Strait song. Jamee would sing a song by Addison Road, a group my family and I had seen perform in Jefferson City only two days before Adam's accident.

Sarah Grinder, a friend of mine who was employed by the church, put together a beautiful collage of Adam's pictures in a power point and set it to music. She contacted me daily to help in any way, and even took me to buy clothes for the funeral.

The ladies of my church and the neighboring Bevier First Baptist Church planned a lunch for the visiting SEALs and our family for the day of the funeral. Many others used their time and talents to help us.

Several people called and offered the hospitality of their homes for visiting family or SEALs to stay during this week. I felt blessed to live in a small town where our grief was shared and lessened by the love and kindness of others. Adam would have been pleased.

August 1, 1987-

> That they may teach the young women to be sober,
> To love their husbands, to love their children,
> --Titus 2:4

"Michele, I'm here for you if you need me," Valarie, my best friend from church, told me one day. I had confided in her about Eric's outbursts.

"What do you mean?" I had expected some remedy for failing marriages, but not what she suggested.

"You can stay with us any time," she answered. "The way things are headed, it's only a matter of time before he gets violent."

"Eric would never hit me," I said defensively. "Well, he has pushed me before, when we were in a fight. And there was the time he was angry enough to kick a basketball at me, barely missing my face."

"That's what I mean. You and the kids may not be safe with him."

All I could think of was how hurt Eric would be when he came home from work to an empty house. I felt sad. But, what if she was right? I had been the recipient of my stepfather's violence. I never wanted my children to live in fear of a parent.

"Maybe you are right," I said in defeat. "What should I do?"

"When you are ready, wait until he leaves for work, and I will come get you."

All the next morning I gave the impression that things were normal. I went through the motions as if in a dream. I fixed Eric's breakfast and packed his lunch, all the time knowing we would be gone when he returned home that evening. He did not suspect a thing. But none of it seemed right.

"I am protecting my babies!" I told myself. "Valarie is a lot wiser than I am. If she thinks we are in danger, maybe we are."

Finally, Eric got into his car and drove away. I remembered one of my stepfather's tricks. He had a habit of disappearing while we were shopping. We would wait in our car with groceries for hours until he came strolling up

40

to leave. One day, as we waited once again, we convinced our mother it would be a good time to get away from his cruelty, and run. She agreed. We drove toward home. Several miles down the road, she came to her senses and returned for him. We all paid dearly for that show of defiance.

"Eric is different," I reasoned. "He is nothing like my stepdad. Or is he?" I called Valarie to come get us.

"Everything will be fine," she reassured me. "My family and I are going out of town for the weekend and you can have the whole house to yourselves."

When they were gone, we sat alone and sad.

"Where's Daddy?" asked Adam. "Is he coming here too?"

"No, Buddy, Daddy is working." Tears were emminent. "Let's just have fun and play some games, OK?" I kept the children busy for the entire day.

When the time drew near for Eric to get home from work, I panicked.

"What will he do? Will he come looking for us? Will he be out of his mind with worry?" I had no answers for the questions that filled my mind. I couldn't make myself call him. The children began to cry. I began to cry. So we went to bed early.

I had only been apart from Eric five times in our marriage: four times when I had been in the hospital delivering babies, and once when I'd gone back to Missouri for a visit. He had called then and begged me to come home early. I'd taken a bus all the way to Louisiana with a toddler and a baby just to be with him.

"Look at me now," I cried after the children had fallen asleep. "Is this what God wants for us?"

I awoke to the sound of someone knocking on a door. Early morning light was streaming through the window. For a moment I did not know where I was. Then I remembered that I was in a bedroom at Valarie's house. The knocking sound came again.

I ran down the stairs and saw Eric outside the front door! How did he know I was here?

"Can you come home now, Shell?" he asked sadly. I rushed to gather the children and leave with him.

He drove us home. We both talked to the children, but

didn't say a word to each other.

Later that evening, when Eric returned home from work, he sat down outside next to a large tree in our yard. I approached him to see if he was alright, and he said the words that would haunt me for years.

"What have I done wrong, Shell?"

Although we had been married for seven years, the avenues of communication between us had never developed. My mind and emotions were so confused that I chose to keep all my worries, disappointment, and anger to myself.

"I'm sorry," I turned and walked away.

September 26, 2010-

> The spirit of a man will sustain his infirmity;
> But a wounded spirit who can bear?
> --Proverbs 18:14

"Can Adam really have been gone for five days now?" Due to lack of sleep and deep sorrow, I felt as if it were still the horrid day I received the call from Amber. Time was passing for everyone around me. But I was, somehow, frozen in grief.

Before I could grasp the reality of it, James and I and several of my children were en route to Columbia, Missouri. The Navy was flying Adam's body into the airport that morning. I was told that a kind businessman had dedicated his jet to transport fallen soldiers to their homes. The weather was windy, cool and overcast. It reflected my gloomy feelings.

"Look at all the motorcycles!" Austen called out from the back seat of our van as we approached the airport. Lined up in front of the drive were around thirty bikers waiting for Adam, too.

They were the Patriot Guard Riders, a nation-wide group that escorts fallen soldiers to their final resting places. These bikers began as a body guard type organization to counteract a group from Kansas who opposes the recent wars by showing up at funerals and gravesites to protest the fact that a young man or woman has given their life for their country. They are the worse kind of traitors, in my opinion. When this cowardly group begins to call out hate-filled statements, the Patriot Guards rev up their motorcycles and drown out what they say.

As we exited our van, several Riders came up to us to pay their respects. I recognized some from Macon County. I was honored to have them there with us.

We were led to a large hanger and asked to wait inside the offices until the jet arrived.

A small group of family and friends were already there. Everyone spoke in hushed tones and shared hugs as we listened for the jet. We did not hear it at all.

Matt entered the room. "He's here. Please come with me."

There inside the hanger sat a beautiful jet. A line of Adam's Navy SEAL friends were standing at attention. They were professional and respectful. Like Adam, they had gone through this ceremony many times for fallen brothers. I knew they felt every loss forever.

Lights began flashing. News reporters were taking pictures. I did not want them there. I wanted to cry openly, but did not want them to have a picture of my grief. I only wanted to share this moment with those who knew Adam and loved him like I did.

I saw someone inside the jet slide his casket forward to the door. There he was, my brave boy! His final flight was over. He was carried with dignity to the waiting hearse.

We returned to our vehicles for the one hour drive back to Macon. Patriot Riders led the way. Our line of cars followed with more Patriot Riders bringing up the rear.

En route, I was amazed at what was happening! Every exit onto the highway through the city was closed off by City Police, Sheriff Departments and Highway Patrol! Most officers were standing outside their vehicles and saluting! I could not hold back the sobs. All this for my son! They did not even know him yet mourned for him! I was no longer so upset with the reporters. My Adam's death was for everyone, so everyone shared our sorrow.

Farther north, on Highway 63, there stood a large American flag painted on a sheet of wood. A family stood in front of it. The parents and children each held small flags and were waving them as we passed by. Several other groups of people were along the way showing respect towards Adam. Who had told that he would be arriving today?

Finally we arrived at the funeral home where Adam would remain for almost another week. Kyle approached as I walked up to the front steps. He said that a group of photographers were in town. They would be in Macon county for days taking pictures of the community. I saw a few of them across the street, laughing and talking. What gave them the right to intrude on our grief? I covered my true feelings and presented a face of stone.

Patriot Guards lined the walkway. We stood outside until Adam was carried into the building, then we followed slowly. Once he was made ready, we filed inside. Chairs were provided for us to rest.

After an hour, the younger children began to get fussy and the older people were expressing some faintness. I wanted to stay with my son. My husband came to the rescue when he announced that everyone was invited to our house for dinner as we had been blessed with more food than we could possibly eat. He bent down to whisper to me to stay as long as I needed to. My love for him welled up inside of me and I hugged him.

Soon everyone had left the room except Eric and I. There we sat in silence, our first born son lying in a casket, only a few feet away from us. The time moved by slowly. I wondered if he was remembering that moment in time, when we were both so surprised we'd had a baby boy. I was wishing I had held on to Adam just a few moments longer when I had felt that last hug from him only a few weeks before this very day.

I'm not sure why I said it, but the words just fell from my lips, "I've never told you this, but, I'm sorry I took the children away from you."

After only a moment of hesitation, he returned with, "I've never told you. I'm sorry I didn't help raise them."

What a shame it took twenty three years and the death of our son for each of us to finally speak from our long-ago-wounded hearts.

October 31, 1987-

Children, obey your parents in the Lord:
For this is right.
--Ephesians 6:1

"Mommy, I want to be a robot for 'trick or treat,'" Adam stated with determination.

"It's called Halloween, Buddy, and we don't have a robot costume. Can't you wear the ninja costume you wore last year?"

"But I wanna be a robot. You can make one, can't you?"

"I'll see what I can do."

"I wished I had never told him about dressing up." I thought to myself as I scoured the house for anything robot-ish looking. "He takes everything so serious!"

I cut out the bottoms of two oatmeal cans, cut a hole into the center of a small box, and cut the top off of a milk carton. Then, I covered everything with aluminum foil. The end result, I determined, looked like the Tin Man costume from the Wizard of Oz movie.

"Good thing he is four. He'll never know"

When it came time to leave, the weather had turned bad with rain and wind. The other children were dressed in their costumes and standing by our front door. I helped Adam step into his "robot" attire. He loved it! With a smile, he took one straight-legged step toward the door and promptly fell flat on his face. The box he wore on his shoulders scraped his neck in the fall. He was finished with trick or treating.

"Get it off me!" he cried.

After several minutes of consoling my wounded 'robot's' feelings, we settled down and agreed that Daddy would go to Macon, rent a movie, and buy some pizza. We would stay home and have a family-fun-night. Every year after that incident I would sew or build the children's costumes weeks in advance.

By that time, Amber and Audrey both were in school. They would come home with stories of the day's lessons and Adam would be so jealous. "I wanna go to school too!" he announced.

"You will, Buddy, but you have to be older." I tried to

reassure him. Inside, I dreaded the thought of he, and Andy, leaving for the biggest part of each day. When my girls began school, I was the one crying in the hallway on the first day. They would be sitting contently with their friends in the classrooms. I couldn't imagine life at home for me when the boys went there too.

To make Adam feel he was not being left behind, I purchased little books at the store and we had our own "lessons." It did not take him long to begin to sound-out words and read! It became his custom to tackle a problem, like reading, until he felt he had mastered it. This habit would serve him well in his future.

I loved being a mother. I felt like it was my greatest calling in life. As a wife, however, I felt like a failure.

Eric was the opposite. His time spent with the babies was limited to, maybe, a few minutes at night. He had given me an ultimatum shortly before Andy was born.

"If you get pregnant again, I'm leaving." His words were almost like jinxing me, if I believed in that.

I was reminded of when, as a teenager, I annoyed my mother so much, that she would often say, "I hope you have six kids, and they're all just like you!"

October 1, 2010-

And he that was dead sat up, and began to speak.
And he delivered him to his mother.
--Luke 7:15

My time with Adam was running out. I had gone only once that week to sit with him at the funeral home. I felt as if I had neglected him. I worried about him, as strange as that seemed. I could not allow myself to think too far beyond each moment.

Sooner than I wanted, the day arrived for his visitation. This would give everyone a chance to pay Adam and our family their respects, before he was buried.

Eric, and some of the children, asked to have an open casket ceremony. I was adamant that I could not handle it.

"You should actually see him before he is buried." I was told by a few well meaning people. "It will be closure for you."

"I don't want 'closure,'" I thought. "I want to remember Adam just as he was."

Only a few weeks before, he had been playing charades with his siblings in our living room. It was his favorite game. He even had the different questions programmed into his phone. I will never forget him standing by the sofa, laughing at the other children when they couldn't guess the phrases. He would act out his words so well that his team guessed them every time. When they got the answer right, he would say, "Boom!" and strut away until his next turn.

I convinced my family to have a private showing of Adam, for those who felt they needed to see him one last time. Two hours before the visitation was to start, I arrived at the church. By the end of the evening, we would have greeted, shaken hands with or hugged over a thousand people. I wanted a few peaceful moments alone with him.

As I sat there before my son's casket, a certain Bible story came into my mind. It had been trying to push its way into my thoughts a few times throughout the past week, but now I finally allowed it to surface.

Once, long ago, when Jesus walked the earth, he came upon a funeral procession. The dead man was the only son of a widow woman. Jesus had compassion on the woman and told her not to cry. He then told the dead son to "arise" and he came back alive! (Luke 7:11-15)

I knew my God has the power to bring the dead back to life. I told myself, "Ask Him!" But even as I said it, I knew I would not ask for Adam to be brought back. Did I have such little faith?

"I know God answers all my prayers." I just knew that the answer would be "no." For some reason, known only to God, Adam was taken from this earth. Who was I to question why?

November 29, 1987-

> For I acknowledge my transgressions:
> And my sin is ever before me.
> --Psalm 51:3

"How much more are we going to torture each other?" I wrote in my journal. "It seems like all Eric and I do now is fight!"

We were members of a coed volleyball team. That was our only time together, without children. By the time we were on our way to the games each week, I would have so much I needed to talk to him about. He saw it as my weekly gripe session. It became a vicious circle of my complaining and his annoyance towards me.

"Maybe I should just kick your butt out. I'm sick of you!" he yelled one particularly trying night after we returned home. I knew just how far to push him, but I had gone that far and beyond.

The word "divorce" entered our vocabulary. The children heard it often. Ironically, I would teach them, years later, "Your word is your bond."

Finally, Eric and I came to an agreement to end our marriage. An eerie feeling of coldness overcame our home. For weeks we spoke very little to each other. Since coming to our decision, we became actually civil and almost respectful in our treatment of one another.

We told our families that we would soon part. No one could convince us to get counseling. Eric's parents were devastated. They sent their pastor to try and convince us of our folly. When he got nowhere with us, he left us by saying, "Well, you're both just stubborn."

I had many moments of doubt about putting my children through a divorce, but then I would be reassured by my friends. "Remember, Michele, Eric could take you all to the temple and be sealed to you. He is choosing not to do so."

I believe that the Lord gave me over to Mormonism. It became my god and I would have it no other way. It even came before my husband.

"I've been thinking, Michele." My friend Valarie told me one day. "Why don't you go to college?"

"I couldn't." I replied. "I have too many children for that right now."

"Just think about it. The girls are in school and I could watch the boys for you."

It didn't take long to convince me. In no time, and without even telling Eric, I was accepted and enrolled at a university forty minutes away from our home.

One day when Eric returned home from work, he said he wanted to talk to me.

"I have something for you." He pulled out a leather-looking case with paper and pen inside. "I thought maybe you could use this." He had known all along of my plans for school.

"I was going to tell you." I choked out the words.

"It's OK." He said and walked into the other room.

There was no Christmas that year for my family. We went through the motions for the children but I hardly decorated or spoke about celebrating. The children felt the sorrow too. They did not ask many questions.

"I can't afford our house payment." I told Valarie one day. "Eric will be staying there."

"I have a rental house in Macon that's empty right now." She told me. "You and the kids can move in as soon as you like."

Could any human ever admit that on Christmas morning 1987, they backed a truck up to their front door and loaded seven years worth of life into it, then drove away? I did that to my family. The repercussions of that act continued for many years.

October 1, 2010-

My sheep hear my voice, and I know them,
and they follow me:
And I give unto them eternal life;
and they shall never perish,
Neither shall any man pluck them out of my hand.
--John 10:27-28

"Michele, the governor is here and he would like to speak to you," Kyle said to me at the visitation. My family and church members were entering the room.

"That's fine." I replied. I felt honored at his visit.

Suddenly, standing in front of me, was Jay Nixon, the Governor of Missouri. It was the first time I had met him. He shook my hand and told me how sorry he was at my loss. Then he presented me with a framed proclamation.

"Michele, out of our gratitude and respect for your son,

Adam's, sacrifice to our country," Governor Nixon read, " I am ordering that the flag of the United States and the flag of Missouri be flown at half-staff at all government buildings statewide for one full day, October 2, 2010. And it shall be flown at half-staff at all government buildings in Macon County from October 3, 2010, to October 8, 2010, from sunrise to sunset."

"Does he know that October eighth is Adam's birthday?" I wondered. I shook his hand again and thanked him for his kindness.

Next, I was told that Representative Tom Shively was at the church and wished to speak to me. I've known Mr. Shively for years. When my brother, Mike and I were in school at North Shelby, Mr. Shively was a teacher there. Our paths have crossed many times and he has always been nice to me. I've even sat in his office at the state capitol and shared my thoughts on being pro life with him.

"Michele, on behalf of the Missouri House of Representatives, we want to extend our heartfelt condolences to you and your family at the loss of your son, Petty Officer Second Class Navy Seal, Adam Olin Smith. We have had a resolution prepared to memorialize Adam's life."

Representative Shively handed me a framed resolution signed by he and the Speaker of the House, Ronald F. Richard. I hugged him. Adam would have been so pleased that two leaders from our great state of Missouri came to show respect for his sacrifice.

Eric and I were led to the front of the room. His wife, Teresa and my husband, James stood at our sides. Eric's parents, Gene and Lucille, also stood up front with us, as well as several of my children. Stools were placed behind us if we needed to sit down. Bottles of water were close by. Then the doors were opened to the public.

Out of the corner of my right eye I could see Adam's flag draped coffin.

"My son is lying there right beside me!" I screamed inwardly. "How can I be expected to bear this pain? Remember, he is with the Lord. That is only his body." I closed my eyes for a moment and pictured my Adam walking with my Lord and asking Him a million questions like he used to ask me as a child. I actually felt peace overtake me and could even smile.

For the next four hours a constant stream of people walked before us. I saw so many of Adam's friends and family members who knew him and loved him. They had come from all over the world to say goodbye.

Adam's cousin, Jarad, and his father, Brian arrived. Jarad and his brother, Jacob had served in Iraq at the same time as Adam and Andy. I had told the boys several times that they should all find each other and have lunch, as if it were a small town like Macon.

Only a couple weeks ago we had received horrible news about Jacob. He had been with the group of soldiers in Iraq who had been attacked after the U.S. had officially declared our combat mission had ended. Two had been killed. Jacob was shot in the leg and, for a few days, we did not know his status.

"How is Jacob doing?" I asked.

"He is doing better, now," answered Brian. "He will be recovering in Hawaii for quite some time."

"I'm so glad," I told him. The line of mourners kept moving so I did not have an opportunity to share any more with them.

There was a strange moment which I wondered later if I had only dreamed that it happened. Someone, a SEAL, came up to me and said, "Mrs. Jorgenson, I want you to meet Jack."

There stood a young man who smiled at me kindly. He apologized for being late. Then he said, "When you're ready for details, I have them."

I did not understand. How could anyone have details? I shook his hand in a daze and the line moved him on.

The night became a blur of faces and tears and hugs and condolences.

"Thank you so much for coming," I repeated over and over again. I truly meant it, but was near exhaustion when the last person passed by me.

"Michele, we need to go home now," my husband said to me. Most everyone else had left. Soon the lights would be turned off and Adam would be left alone again! I wanted to sleep there for the night.

"He's in Heaven now," I reminded myself once again. "He is not here."

March 4, 1988-

> If I regard iniquity in my heart,
> the Lord will not hear me:
> --Psalm 66:18

Our first night in Valarie's rental house had been a nightmare. It was freezing outside and I was not smart enough to work the furnace. I burnt myself repeatedly trying to light the wood stove in the dining room. Finally, the fire began to blaze and warmth returned to our bodies. I made a pallet of blankets right in front of the stove on the floor and the children and I all huddled there in the huge old empty house and cried. Crying was the way I ended many nights. Yet, time moves on even as we mourn.

"I miss Eric! It's been two months since we parted and I'm still crying for him."

I lost twenty pounds. I could hardly eat or sleep and was struggling halfway through my first semester of college. I was also trying to maintain my sanity and be a good mommy. It was difficult for all of us. Our carefree sunny days of long walks and made-up stories and laughter seemed to have come to an end.

Adam was the most inquisitive about our situation. From the first night, he wanted to know why we weren't going home. My heart broke for him. He constantly asked when we were going to see his daddy.

Eric, at first, told me he wanted the children every weekend. He did not want to set up any visitation arrangements through the court. But, as I showed up at his doorstep each Saturday morning, he became less and less excited to have them with him.

Once he came to visit me. We had a long talk after the children had gone to sleep. We told each other how much we missed being a family. We decided to try and work out our marriage! I allowed him to stay for several hours. After all, we were still married. He said he would come over the next night for dinner and we could tell the children.

The next day at school I was happier than I had been for months. I would pick up the children and fix a nice dinner for them and Eric. Everything went as planned that evening. The children were all cleaned up. The house was picked up and tidy. I had prepared everything I could that I knew Eric liked to eat. We all waited with high expectations for the sound of his footsteps on the porch.

Thirty minutes after he was supposed to be there, I finally called him.

"Eric," I questioned. "Where are you? I have dinner ready for you."

Without hesitation Eric said, "It's not going to work out, Shell."

"Do you mean you can't make it tonight?" I played dumb.

"No, you and I won't work out. We've tried it already. You know we will just fight all the time like we did before. I'm sorry, Shell."

I fought back the tears as I returned to the four children who sat waiting hopefully for their parents to be sitting at the same table.

"Guess what," I lied, "Daddy had to work tonight so he can't make it to eat with us."

"Can he come here tomorrow?" asked Adam disappointedly.

"I don't know, Buddy, we'll see. Now let's eat all this food. I worked hard on this meal."

No matter how much I chewed each bite, I could not seem to swallow it well. After a few attempts, I stopped eating and just made sure the children ate.

I struggled impatiently to get the children to go to bed. Finally the last question was answered. The last prayer was said. The last hug and "I love you" was given. And, the last child, Adam, dozed off while asking for another story. I was alone with my thoughts.

If it is possible for a woman to feel used by her own husband, I felt it that night. I realized that Eric had had no intention of coming back to us.

"Why would he?" I thought in anger. "Who wants to come home each night to a nagging wife, a house full of kids, bills to pay, and responsibility?"

My anger turned to self pity, then to sadness.

"How can I go on without my Eric?" I cried. "I will never love anyone like that again! It hurts too much! From now on, I will only live for my children!"

October 2, 2010-

For I am persuaded, that neither death,
nor life, nor angels, nor principalities, nor powers,
nor things present, nor things to come, nor height, nor
depth, nor any other creature,
shall be able to separate us from the love of God,
which is in Christ Jesus our Lord.
                                    --Romans 8:38-39

Before I could open my eyes that morning, I felt sadness
wash over me. I was still alive.

"This is it," I thought. "Today Adam will be lowered
into the dark Earth and buried." I felt as if great weights
had been attached to my body. I could not lift myself up
from the bed.

"Please, Father, help me." I prayed. "You said you
wouldn't give us more than we could handle! How strong
do you think I am?"

Somehow, I managed to get dressed. I was glad I had
chosen the pant suit instead of the skirt. It was a cold and
windy fall day. In contrast, the sun shone brightly. James
told me he would get the children ready and meet me at the
church if I liked. He had been such a source of strength this
entire week and a half.

As I drove myself to the church, I could see hundreds
of Patriot Guards already gathering around it. I felt safer
because of them.

Inside, I was able to sit one last time with the body of
my fallen son. I spoke to him in whispers. "You did it,
Buddy! You're life is done now. No more tears or pain or
suffering for you. Now you can rest."

I remembered talking with Adam about a year ago,
soon after he had re-enlisted into the SEALs. He sat at my
kitchen table and confided in me that all the men he looked
up to were gone or retired. This made him the one that
others came to for guidance. He looked so very tired for a
moment.

"I bet you have to fake it a lot, don't you," I joked. We
laughed as he agreed with me. We both knew that he had
years of experience and training behind him which made
him the best choice of a leader for the younger men. Still,

I wondered how long a human can run at high speed a hundred percent of the time?

Many of the SEALs had arrived at the church. I watched as they stood around in groups and spoke quietly. Then I saw Jack. I could not wait any longer. I had to know what he knew about Adam's death. I waited until he was in the hallway and went to him.

"I'm ready for those details," I told him.

He took me to the end of the hall and told me about my son's accident.

"I was in the helicopter right behind Adam's."

I hadn't known there were more than one helicopter! I had been wondering if Adam had been conscious or in pain for hours before help had arrived too late.

"We saw a flash of light and didn't know what it was until dispatch radioed that a chopper was down. I knew it was Adam's. I tried to reach him but there was no answer. We landed about eight hundred meters from him.

"I ran to the first person I saw," Jack continued. "It wasn't Adam. This guy was still alive but badly injured. Others came to help him. Then someone yelled, 'I found Adam!'

While Jack told me of the horrible scene he had witnessed, his eyes never left mine. I don't know what feelings were revealed by my expression, but Jack reached out and took my hand before he continued. I could see that it hurt him deeply to relive the tragedy but he did it for my peace of mind.

"When I got there, he looked like he was just asleep. He was leaning up against some rocks with his eyes closed. I couldn't believe he was gone until I searched for a pulse.

"There wasn't a mark on him. Later I think someone said a bump formed on his head."

"What?" I screamed inwardly.

This information confirmed what the coroner had found. It was what I had been hoping, too. My son had just hit his head on something and died. It must have been instant!

"My Lord and my God, could it be that in the middle of this horrendous pain You have shown me Your control and compassion?"

A couple of Jack's friends had come up to us, not knowing the importance of this one conversation to me. It ended abruptly. But, it never ended for me.

After all the years of working ambulance, now I understood why family members will almost hound you for details of a loved one's accident. You just need to know.

"Michele, the ladies have a lunch ready for you and your family," Kyle told me gently. I followed him downstairs.

The ladies of the Macon and Bevier First Baptist churches had outdone themselves. A huge buffet had been set up in the basement with enough tables for everyone. Many family members, SEALs and friends who had traveled from all over the world were gathering there to eat and fellowship. I could not eat a thing. I latched onto one of my grand-babies and walked around to see if everyone had what they needed.

My two brothers, Michael and Ronald came. We are not a close family. We sometimes joke that the McPhersons never get together except at funerals. It is almost the truth. I was glad to see them both.

James came to me and said, "I want to show you something."

We went upstairs and to a side exit of the church. He was about to go outside.

"Wait a minute," I cautioned him, "Are you sure we should go out there?"

"I don't think anyone will notice us if we go out a side door. Besides, you won't believe this."

Curiosity overruled my caution and I went out the door. We didn't have to go far. There, right outside the church, were hundreds of Patriot Guards lined up on both sides of the front street. Each held a flag and pole which rested on the ground. They were a sight I will never forget.

Later I received a card in the mail from one of the guards, Kate Blaise. I had met her a few years before when we had both been invited to speak to my youngest daughter's second grade class. I told the class about my two military sons and she told them about her husband who had been killed in a brown out just like Adam's. My heart broke for her but I was very impressed with how she handled the questions of the children. How ironic.

In her sympathy card she included an essay she had written titled, *The Flags*. It was a description of the scene outside the church while I was inside. She thought I might like to know. I will be forever grateful to her for all she has done for me and our country.

As James and I turned to go back inside the church someone called my name. I turned around to see a woman I knew from Bevier. She came running across the street to hug me. Then she hurried back to her place in line with the Patriot Guards.

We took a back stairwell to the basement. Most of the people had gone up to the gym where the funeral would be held. But I wasn't ready.

I stalled as long as I could. All my children were up there and seated. Finally my husband said I needed to go upstairs. I told him to go ahead. I made it to the top of the stairs. There, I sat on a bench in the hall outside the doors. I did not want to go inside.

"Michele, the Commodore would like to meet you," Matt stood in front of me with a kind looking gentleman. I just felt as if I should stand up and shake his hand.

"I can see where your son received his strength," he said kindly. I thanked him as he told me how sorry he was about Adam. He went to take his place at the front of the room.

"It's time to go in, Michele," said James.

The room was full. I was the last to enter. I held tight to his arm as he led me to my seat. In front of me was my Adam's casket. The video of his life was projected on the screen above him. The children had found pictures I hadn't seen in years. Some of his Navy friends had contributed pictures I had never seen before.

I felt faint. I prayed for strength to get through this, all the time wishing it would never end. That would be too final.

March 7, 1988-

> But and if she depart, let her remain unmarried,
> Or be reconciled to her husband: and let not the husband
> put away his wife.
> --1 Corinthians 7:11

I was barely functioning through my depression. Not only did I turn my life over to Mormonism, I gave all control over my life to my Mormon friends and "superiors." They gladly accepted. I felt low and unworthy to make my own decisions.

My friends and I had been through the Mormon temple in Chicago several times together. There, we made covenants and took blood oaths. Although it was only symbolic, it was still very serious stuff. Telling the secrets of the temple would be worse than death.

Although I was still married to Eric, it seemed to have become a goal for my church friends to find my next husband for me. After all, it was Eric's lack of holding the priesthood that kept him from taking his family to the Celestial Kingdom, or heaven.

There were only three eligible men in our branch with whom I could be paired. One man was tall and very handsome. But he was also very childish and wild. Valarie did not think he would suit me. Another was three years younger than me. He was Brigham Young University bound, and his family certainly did not want him getting interested in me and my four children. Finally there was Jeffrey, quiet, dark and brooding. He was chosen for my priesthood holding husband.

Adam took the separation of his parents the hardest. He became whiney and more and more demanding. At times I lost my temper and yelled at him. I wasn't actually upset with him, but with myself. He was just the little reminder that I was really still married to my first love, his father. He was like the voice of reasoning and truth. Often, he surprised me with his questions and comments.

"Mommy, were we born bad and someone just taught us to be good?" he asked me one day.

"No, Buddy," I answered, "we were born good and the devil wants us to be bad. It's my job to help you chose good over bad until you are old enough to tell the difference." That seemed to satisfy him for the moment.

Although Adam was not the oldest child, he quickly rose in rank to leader. Even at age five, he began to rule over his older sisters, and had won an everlasting loyalty from Andy. It wasn't meanness that drove them to follow him, but rather his strong personality.

I too, wanted to gain his respect. I quickly learned that he despised being mocked. One of his greatest dislikes was finding out that he had been pronouncing a word wrong for any period of time. He hated to be laughed at, no matter how cute his mispronunciation was.

"Mommy, look at that B-truck," he pointed out the car window one day.

"You mean that big truck over there?" I questioned.

"It's a B-truck, right?"

"It's actually a big truck. You just couldn't say "big" when you were small so you called it B."

"You mean there are no B-trucks?"

"No, I'm sorry."

He was so shocked. It did not take long for him to realize that we had been laughing every time he said the wrong words. He was furious. He did not forget that humiliation for a long time. I was glad he did not remember he had once called elevators "alligators." After that day I made sure to correct him every time he mispronounced a word.

October 2, 2010-

> And God shall wipe away all tears from their eyes;
> And there shall be no more death,
> neither sorrow, nor crying,
> Neither shall there be any more pain:
> for the former things are passed away.
> --Revelation 21:4

Finally, the music stopped and the room fell silent.

Pastor John stood up. "We'd like to welcome you today as we celebrate the life of Adam Smith. You've noticed, there is a candle lit today. This is a candle that our church lights every Sunday morning in observance of our soldiers that are fighting for our country and to uphold the truth."

That candle had meant so much to me over the past few years. Each Sunday I watched its small glowing light as it flickered behind the preacher. I would instantly take into account where my older sons were in the world. Then I would say an extra prayer for them. Today, it hurt my heart to look at it.

My attention was called back to the present.

"Please stand as the national anthem is sung," Pastor John asked. I had never heard it sung as a duet. It was astounding.

I noticed who was sitting behind the pastors: many of Adam's friends who were SEALs, a row of Army buddies of Andy's, an Admiral, a General, a Commander, Representative Shively and more.

When the song finished Pastor John led in prayer.

"Dear Heavenly Father, You are the Creator of life and the Author of our salvation. In Thee do we trust and find our hope in You. We recognize that we are mere men and women in need of a Savior who is Jesus Christ our Lord, Your Son, who gave himself up to be our sacrifice for our sin, buried and rose again. And for those who call upon His name and believe, to them have been given the right to become the children of God.

"Lord today we gather in Your name and in the truth of Your Word. Though our hearts be broken, yet we are not crushed, we are perplexed, but not in despair, struck down, but not destroyed. Because You are the Lifter of our head. You are our Shield and Strength, our Portion, Deliverer, our Shelter, Strong Tower, our very present Help in time of need.

"Father, we pray for strength today for Adam's family and for the days ahead. And pray that if someone does not know You as their Personal Savior that they will, today, accept You into their life.

"We give You praise in Your name. Amen."

When Pastor John sat down, Matt Carrolll stood to sing. As he'd promised, it was the George Strait song he had searched for and found! It told about taking a "road less travelled." It was a perfect example of Adam! How he would go off into the unknown and do so bravely. It was not the choice for the "faint of heart."

I started to hyperventilate. I had to consciously slow down my breathing and focus on getting through this day.

Next, Commander Symenski spoke. He told how Matt's song had been very fitting for Adam. He spoke of Adam's bravery and the ways of the Navy SEALs. He said this was the third in a series of funerals they had attended, yet it never gets easier. He explained about the terrible conditions in Afghanistan, the environment, the terrain and

60

the enemies.

"In Afghanistan, there are no routine movements or patrols. Every operation is on the margin of physical human endurance and mechanical performance due to the extreme weather patterns, indomitable terrain and distances. The enemy is just as indomitable and fierce.

"In the black of the night, almost a week and a half ago now, Adam and his teammates took the strength of their friendship, and bond of shared experience and arduous training, cast aside their fears and doubts, and climbed into the Army Blackhawk helicopter. They were physically and mentally prepared to persevere in the weather and terrain, engage the enemy, and carry out their mission."

The Commander continued, "Once the accident occurred, the mission changed instantly to retrieve and rescue everyone from Adam's helicopter. This was done with respect and order and compassion." He spoke very highly of my Adam. His words were comforting to me.

Jamee stood up and sang "What Do I Know of Holy?" Her voice and the words reached down to my very soul.

I was sorry if it was sad for some. To me it described how I felt at that time in regard to my Heavenly Father. I had been counseling Him for so long and giving Him my "grocery list" of to-dos as if He worked for me! Then, in a blink of an eye, He had the power to reach down and pluck one of my very own babies off of this earth!

Who am I?

March 9, 1988-

> For the Lord hath called thee like a woman
> forsaken and grieved in spirit,
> and a wife of youth, when thou wast refused,
> saith thy God.
> --Isaiah 54:6

"I was divorced today," I wrote with a shaking hand in my journal.

I had been told to arrive early at the court house. Then I had to sit through several other court cases. I learned that a person could go to prison for having only a couple grams of marijuana on him. (I think he may have done more than that, but that was the final mistake.)

There were a few people I knew at the court house. They were there in support of others. That is what happens when you live in a small community, everyone knows your business.

I let my mind wonder to the past two months. They had sped by so quickly.

"Shouldn't we extend this separation or something?" I had asked myself and others, several times. No one thought it would be a good idea.

I actually confided, one rare time, in my mother. "I'm just so depressed about this whole thing."

"You'll be alright," she answered, "the first divorce is always the hardest."

I did not speak to her about it again.

The noisy door to the court room opened, snapping me back to the present.

"Eric?" I sat up straighter. It wasn't him.

I imagined how embarrassing it would be, yet romantic, when he would come bursting into the room to stop this whole horrid business. Each time the door opened my hope for that scene lessened.

My Mormon lawyer arrived. He informed me that Eric did not have to appear in court.

"What?" I cried inwardly. "Our final act together and he makes me do it alone!"

I rose when I was told to, and moved to the front of the room. I was sworn in and sat next to the kind judge. Fighting back tears, I answered all his questions.

He then gave the judgment, "divorce granted."

I went through the motions of thanking my lawyer and fled home.

Alone, I was able to weep without witnesses. I felt as if someone close to me had died. In a sense, I reasoned, it was worse than that. Someone I loved did not love me anymore! I couldn't bear the thought of my Eric ever being in someone else's arms.

I dried my tears and drove to pick up my children at Valarie's. How could I look at their sweet little faces?

always, I had my dear journals. Yet, somehow I feared that these words may seem too personal. I just wanted others to get a glimpse of the man we all knew and loved.

It was too late to change my mind. Pastor John stood to read what I had written.

"About Adam- from his brothers and sisters memories, and from his mother's journals:

"Adam did not enter easily into this world. He had wrapped his umbilical cord twice around his neck and made the doctor use forceps to extract him. (He came out very blue....)"

Pastor John told the crowd about Adam staying an extra night in the hospital with yellow jaundice, and of his rolling over at an early age, and about his three-year-old concerns of changing the world.

"For a time," Pastor John continued, "Adam had a fear of loud noises. During thunderstorms, his mother would have to sit straight up on his bed until the storm passed. All parades and fireworks had to be watched from inside shelter."

"Adam's weekends were spent watching his favorite cartoon, Duck Tails, playing with his brother and sisters, and having sleepovers with his best buddies, Obie and Clark."

"Adam hadn't attended Kindergarden very long when he decided to drop out. He was already reading and doing simple math so it just didn't hold his attention."

"Adam is the third member of the 'A-Team'. Namely: Amber, Audrey, Adam, Andy, Abbie, Allie, Anna, Austen and Angel. Although he was not the oldest, he quickly rose in rank to a leadership position. He ruled the others with fear and love. The children knew if Adam curled his tongue in his mouth and came after them, they had better run. He could wait forever for them if they locked themselves in the bathroom."

"Long ago, Adam's mom thought she could write poetry. So, while the children slept or played, she wrote poems about each one. This is what she wrote to Adam when he was six."

Today He is Mine

Right now he is mine,
My own little one
Who lovingly lives close to me,
But one day another will capture his heart,
And second his mother will be,
And second his mother will be.

So, as for now,
These moments I have
To spend with my dear precious son,
I'll color his books and play in his games,
Knowing one day he'll be gone,
Knowing one day he'll be gone.

"Journal entry September 29, 1992-

"My Adam Olin will be nine years old in about one week! What a challenge he has been, and yet, what a joy. My whole soul wants to do nothing but make his life easy. Yet, I fear he faces a life full of struggle and pain. So I must, as all mothers should do with their sons, begin to loosen the strings that bind him to me, so that some day he might soar higher than I ever dreamed."

"He feels I am so very hard on him, with duties and so forth around our home, and, he is right. I don't want him to be a bitter and cruel man, but I wish for him to stand tall and walk straight, never wavering, until the end of his days."

"His mind is capable of leading others who may be weaker than he.

"He will do well."

June 1, 1988-

Neither is there salvation in any other:
For there is none other name under heaven
given among men,
Whereby we must be saved.
--Acts 4:12

October 2, 2010-

No weapon that is formed against thee shall prosper;
and every tongue that shall rise against thee
in judgment thou shalt condemn.
This is the heritage of the servants of the Lord,
and their righteousness is of me, saith the Lord.
--Isaiah 54:17

The echo of Jamee's voice still rang in our ears as Jack stood to speak.

"I was lucky enough to know Adam, Adam Olin Smith." (Adam was always so proud of his middle name, Olin, that he would often introduce himself using his full name. Jack must have remembered that.)

"I've been with Adam since I started BUD/S. There aren't very many people here who haven't gone through BUD/S with Adam." Some laughter was heard coming from the SEALs. (This comment was made in remembrance of the many times Adam had been rolled back to the next class, during BUD/S, because of illness or injury.)

"Adam was lucky enough to get through Hell Week before I did. But that didn't change him. He never treated me any different. That's just the way Adam was. It didn't matter who you were or what you did, he treated you like a man. And he expected the same."

"Someone a lot smarter than me wrote this:

"Build me a son, oh Lord,
Who will be strong enough to know
    when he is weak,
And brave enough to face himself
    when he is afraid.
One who will be proud and unbending
    in honest defeat,
And humble and gentle in victory."
                (General Douglas MacArthur.)

"Adam was humble about ninety nine percent of the time. The other one percent of the time he was beating me in HALO and Madden. And, since we were the only two

63

white guys on teams that could play basketball, we always went out together. And we took it to everybody."

"Adam was a son, a brother, a boyfriend and a team mate. And he was our best friend. He will always be a Horseman. He'll never be forgotten."

"I'm gonna miss you, Brother." With that, Jack took his seat.

Pastor Scott rose to read Adam's obituary. His voice broke and he could not regain his composure. Pastor John read it for him.

"SO2 Navy SEAL, Adam Olin Smith, age 26, of Bevier, Missouri, was killed in action on Tuesday, September 21, 2010, when the helicopter he was traveling in crashed in Zabul Province in southern Afghanistan."

"Adam was born October 8, 1983, in Baton Rouge, Louisiana. He is the son of Eric Smith and Michele (McPherson) Jorgenson. He graduated from Bevier High School in 2002. Adam enlisted in the United States Navy on October 27, 2004. After completion of Recruit Training in Great Lakes, Illinois, he reported to Naval Air Technical Training Command in Pensacola, Florida. He then reported to Basic Underwater Demolition/SEAL training at Naval Special Warfare Center in Coronado, California on March 23, 2005. He graduated from BUD/S on August 2007 with class 259. Petty Officer Smith was assigned to SEAL Team FOUR, at Little Creek, Virginia."

"His awards include a Bronze Star, Navy and Marine Corps Commendation Medal, Joint Service Achievement Medal, Navy and Marine Corps Achievement Medal, National Defense Service Medal, Afghanistan Campaign Medal, Iraq Campaign Medal, Global War on Terrorism Expeditionary Medal, Global War on Terrorism Service Medal, Sea Service Deployment Ribbon, Navy Rifleman Expert Medal, and Navy Pistol Shot Expert Medal."

"Petty Officer Smith is survived by his parents, Eric and Michele, his brothers, Andrew, Austen and Zachary, and his sisters, Amber, Audrey, Abigail, Alaina, Anna, Angel and Lindsey. He was preceded in death by his great Grandfather, Harvey Olin Blackorby and Grandfather, Gordon Keith McPherson."

Pastor John sat down. Once again Pastor Scott stood to speak. Once again, he could not get control.

"Pastor John, can you read Michele's writings?"

April 14, 1988-

This is a faithful saying, and worthy of all acceptation,
That Christ Jesus came into the world to save sinners;
Of whom I am chief.
--1 Timothy 1:15

I had been "seeing" Jeffrey for nearly a month. My journal read like a mad woman with a double personality. Many times I doubted my feelings for this man. Many times my doubts were put to rest.

"I know what you should do," suggested Valarie. "You need to talk to Brother Robertson from Kirksville. He has been married before and has a great family. He is very spiritual and he will guide you the right way."

But I knew I could not speak with him, as I was too shy. He was on the staff of the college.

Then a strange thing happened.

The next week, when I was in Kirksville, my car would not start after school. I did not know what to do. I remembered what Valarie had said and went to Brother Robertson. Of course he would help me. That is what all good Mormons do. They are there for each other.

We had quite a walk to his car. It took some time jump starting mine. I just knew that Heavenly Father had arranged for my car not to start so that I could have this meaningful talk with such a wise man.

I told him of my painful divorce and of being alone now with four little children. I told him of this whirlwind courtship, and now talk of marriage, with Jeffrey.

"I know what you're trying to do," he answered. I felt as if he could read my thoughts. It worried me that he would see my true feelings and be displeased. "You're trying to get over your first marriage before you get married again."

"That's true!" I told him, excited that he knew my doubts.

"Don't do that."

"What?" I asked confused.

"Part of healing is to move on."

"Ok," I agreed. "Thank you for the help and advice."

65

Somehow, I did not feel comfort at his permission to rush into another marriage. Later I found out that his first marriage had ended when his wife died. He had known she loved him. That is quite different from divorce. Also, I found out he had waited two whole years before he remarried! I should have asked more questions.

To confirm the advice of Brother Robertson, I decided one evening to ask my Home Teacher. A Home Teacher is a man chosen by the leaders of the Mormon Church to come to your home once a month (with his wife) to teach a lesson. Also, he is to see if there are any unmet needs in your family.

When Brother Schultz finished his lesson, I put him to the test by asking what I should do with my life. I told him of my uneasiness at the impending marriage.

He agreed with Brother Robertson. He said he has a philosophy. "If they both want it to, any man can marry any woman and make it work."

There, I had it! Two of the most spirit filled people on the planet agreed. It must be a go.

Instead of taking a poll on the subject I asked just one more important man in my life.

"Adam, can Mommy marry Jeffrey?"

"No."

"Why?"

"I want my other Daddy back."

Out of the mouths of babes!

October 2, 2010-

The righteous perisheth, and no man layeth it to heart:
    And merciful men are taken away,
        none considering that the righteous
        is taken away from the evil to come.
He shall enter into peace: they shall rest in their beds,
        each one walking in his uprightness.
                    --Isaiah 57:1-2

Suddenly I felt very nervous.

I had asked the children for certain memories they had of our Adam and had gotten several responses. And, as

66

always, I had my dear journals. Yet, somehow I feared that these words may seem too personal. I just wanted others to get a glimpse of the man we all knew and loved.

It was too late to change my mind. Pastor John stood to read what I had written.

"About Adam- from his brothers and sisters memories, and from his mother's journals:

"Adam did not enter easily into this world. He had wrapped his umbilical cord twice around his neck and made the doctor use forceps to extract him. (He came out very blue....)"

Pastor John told the crowd about Adam staying an extra night in the hospital with yellow jaundice, and of his rolling over at an early age, and about his three-year-old concerns of changing the world.

"For a time," Pastor John continued, "Adam had a fear of loud noises. During thunderstorms, his mother would have to sit straight up on his bed until the storm passed. All parades and fireworks had to be watched from inside shelter."

"Adam's weekends were spent watching his favorite cartoon, Duck Tails, playing with his brother and sisters, and having sleepovers with his best buddies, Obie and Clark."

"Adam hadn't attended Kindergarden very long when he decided to drop out. He was already reading and doing simple math so it just didn't hold his attention."

"Adam is the third member of the 'A-Team'. Namely: Amber, Audrey, Adam, Andy, Abbie, Allie, Anna, Austen and Angel. Although he was not the oldest, he quickly rose in rank to a leadership position. He ruled the others with fear and love. The children knew if Adam curled his tongue in his mouth and came after them, they had better run. He could wait forever for them if they locked themselves in the bathroom."

"Long ago, Adam's mom thought she could write poetry. So, while the children slept or played, she wrote poems about each one. This is what she wrote to Adam when he was six."

Today He is Mine

Right now he is mine,
My own little one
Who lovingly lives close to me,
But one day another will capture his heart,
And second his mother will be,
And second his mother will be.

So, as for now,
These moments I have
To spend with my dear precious son,
I'll color his books and play in his games,
Knowing one day he'll be gone,
Knowing one day he'll be gone.

"Journal entry September 29, 1992-

"My Adam Olin will be nine years old in about one week! What a challenge he has been, and yet, what a joy. My whole soul wants to do nothing but make his life easy. Yet, I fear he faces a life full of struggle and pain. So I must, as all mothers should do with their sons, begin to loosen the strings that bind him to me, so that some day he might soar higher than I ever dreamed."

"He feels I am so very hard on him, with duties and so forth around our home, and, he is right. I don't want him to be a bitter and cruel man, but I wish for him to stand tall and walk straight, never wavering, until the end of his days."

"His mind is capable of leading others who may be weaker than he.

"He will do well."

June 1, 1988-

Neither is there salvation in any other:
For there is none other name under heaven
given among men,
Whereby we must be saved.
--Acts 4:12

I awoke suddenly from a horrible nightmare. I had been chased by something evil through the entire night. I was running down a dark street, looking back over my shoulder, when I slammed forcefully into someone. I turned to say I was sorry, but realized I was facing two strong arms crossed in anger. I slowly looked up to see a beast with the head of a dog on a man. The eyes pierced through me with pure hate. I knew I was looking into the face of Satan! I began to scream and cry.

Suddenly I was shaken awake by my two friends Valarie and Lisa. It finally dawned on me that we were all three in a hotel room, just blocks away from the Chicago temple. This was my wedding day!

I calmed down and told them about my nightmare.

"Oh," Lisa said, "we were thinking you had decided not to marry Jeffrey after all."

"Why would they think that?" I wondered, hiding my surprise.

Several of my friends had driven a long way with us to witness this marriage. (Only worthy members of the Church of Jesus Christ of Latter Day Saints can attend any temple ceremony.) Even Jeffrey must be worthy. With these thoughts, I continued with the wedding preparations.

We had many plans for our honeymoon. We were going to stay somewhere near the Great Lakes, taking several days to tour and spend time together. Once the wedding ended and our friends headed back to Missouri, Jeffrey realized he had not brought enough money for the honeymoon. Not so much disappointed as confused, I agreed we should spend one night in Springfield, Illinois then return home. I missed my children!

Our next full day home we took my children to the Saint Louis Zoo. They had a good time. Adam accidently opened Jeffrey's camera and ruined the entire roll of film. I think it was an accident. I was impressed that Jeffrey did not yell at us.

We spent the next day moving Jeffrey's things into my house in Macon. The man saved everything! He had lived in Cairo, Missouri and worked even farther away in Moberly. He would commute thirty minutes each day to work.

I had been interested in a farm that Valarie owned, but

she and her husband, Paul did not think it was a good idea to sell it to a single woman with children. It was just too far out into the country. It was ideally located between Macon and Cairo. Now that Jeffrey and I were married, they agreed that my family could move there. It needed some fixing up though. Jeffrey made the down payment from his savings. The price of the farm was only ten thousand dollars. It was ten acres!

Then I witnessed the men of the Church at their finest. They announced on Sunday that we needed a work day to get our house ready to move into. It was set for the next Saturday. Many of the men showed up with their own tools. It was a time that a woman might call "too many cooks in the kitchen!" No one was in charge. There was no plan at all.

Some men started in the kitchen, putting up beams to lower the ceiling. Jeffrey had purchased the sheet rock and lumber himself. Unfortunately, he bought treated lumber that should be used outside, at a more expensive price. They used it in the kitchen anyway.

Another man decided that the chimney on the house was too unstable. He climbed up onto the roof and knocked it down. Now the stove could not be used at all. There would be no heat in the winter until another chimney could be built.

Still others felt that the bathroom wasn't in working order. They got together and removed the toilet and left a huge hole in the floor!

Each act of destruction was actually necessary. Yet, without a plan to reconstruct, we had more of a mess and trouble. Soon we were left alone with no knowledge of how to rebuild our house.

With Paul's help, somehow we fixed the bathroom, finished the kitchen ceiling, and began to live there. As we worked on the house, Adam and Andy wanted to help, too. I would start several nails in scrap pieces of wood and let them finish nailing them. They were probably the most dedicated men on the job.

Jeffrey's brother Bob was married to a wonderful outdoorsy woman named Carol. She had a farm which she ran herself. She brought over goats, chickens and even two little ponies for me! The kids and I loved it there.

Jeffrey was gone to work or to the National Guard a lot. So I could have lived there alone with my children. I milked goats, butchered chickens, drew water from a cistern, built gates and fences, and more. I even built a tree house for the children.

We spent many hours reading in our tree house, taking care of the animals or going for long walks and exploring. The children thrived.

Our country had been having trouble with Iran at that time. A jet had been shot down. But that was not our concern. The world couldn't touch my family. Not on our little farm.

October 2, 2010-

The steps of a good man are ordered by the Lord:
And he delighteth in his way.
Though he fall, he shall not be utterly cast down:
For the Lord upholdeth him with his hand.
--Psalm 37: 23-24

I wanted everyone at the funeral to know the orneriness yet sense of humor of my Adam.

Pastor John went on, "One day when Adam was about twelve, his mother noticed the house was quiet. That could only mean trouble, so she went in search of the children.

"She looked out a back window in time to see Adam, lining his little sisters up by a mud puddle. Then he had his brother, Andy, swing into them with a tire swing, knocking them into the mud!

"She threw the window up and began to yell when Adam hollered back, 'Mom, they like it!' Then she noticed they were all laughing, including the muddy girls."

"One Christmas, Adam came downstairs and told the other children that Mom said they could go ahead and open their gifts. As they all ripped into the gifts with their names on them, they didn't notice Adam sitting there quietly, with his gifts unopened. When his mother came down, they were all in trouble, including Adam."

"Adam did help throw rocks through an old store-front window in Excello. And he would never have confessed, except he was told his fingerprints were lifted from the rocks. (His mother wishes to apologize to the Macon County Sheriff's Department for yelling at them that HER children wouldn't do such a thing.)"

As laughter filled the room, I realized that telling others about Adam's childhood was a good thing to lighten everyone's hearts, mine included. After all, we were there to celebrate the life of my son. And what a life he led!

Pastor John told them that Adam would lick all the crescent rolls on a plate to keep the others from wanting any. He called his little sisters 'The Rat Pack' and told them he would play "army" with them. Then he would take them into another room, line them up, and tell them to stand at attention until he returned. They would remain there for the longest time while he went off to play video games or watch TV.

"Adam spent a few years on the fish farm." Pastor John read. "He became a hard worker and strong swimmer. It is a place he loved."

The fish farm was still a sensitive subject for me, as that was the home of my third husband. Yet, this day was not about me. It was about my Adam.

While on the fish farm, I had allowed Adam to borrow my car to drive the twenty miles to school. I was out in the garden when I began to hear the loudest muffler noise coming from the direction of town. Finally, I could see my only car coming down the gravel road. Adam had been ramping hills with my car after school and had drug off everything possible underneath it, including the muffler. Pastor John told the story.

He also told of one time that Adam had helped drive his grandparents from Louisiana to Missouri. He had tried to throw his chewing gum out the window, when it became stuck. In his effort to free it, he ran off the road, spun completely around in the median, and came to a stop on the opposite shoulder, facing the oncoming traffic. He did not ask to drive again on that trip.

Adam had several run-ins with the law as a teenager. Pastor John read of one such incident.

"Adam and his friends had decided to go mailbox bashing one night. He didn't realize that one of the boxes destroyed was that of his own Aunt and Uncle. It was

72

decided that a "sleepover" would help him straighten up. (His mother wishes to apologize again to the Macon County Sheriff's Department for calling them every fifteen to thirty minutes to check on her son.)

Everyone laughed, but I remembered how worried I was for the boy. I was grateful that God had protected him that night. I felt sure He had bigger plans for Adam.

July 17, 1988-

So teach us to number our days,
that we may apply our hearts unto wisdom.
--Psalm 90:12

What wonderful children I have! I love them all so much.

First there is Amber Marie, who is seven and a half. She is such a lady. She recently had her ears pierced and must wear dresses almost every day. The child is my little genius! She practically taught herself to read, and now reads better than some adults. But that is a mother's opinion.

Then there is Audrey Loraine who is now six and a half. She is very sweet and loving. I have never seen a child so young who loves babies so much. She would be happy if I could have twins and give her one!

Next is Adam Olin, who is almost five. He is my little man! For a four year old, he seems very concerned with spiritual things. Some of his questions are too deep for me to answer, about life and death and beyond. I feel he will be a great, kind leader some day.

Finally, there is Andrew Lee, who just turned three last month. What a challenge! The child is almost bigger than Adam and doesn't seem to feel pain much. Twice he has come close to dying on this farm. And twice he has been miraculously spared. What has God planned for him to do with his life? I just need to keep him safe.

I imagined that I would not be having any more children. When Eric told me he did not want to have any more babies, I had my tubes tied. I was told by the doctor that any time the tubes are even messed with it will probably sterilize the woman.

But now I am married to a Mormon. Mormons are commanded to multiply and build up the Kingdom. I feel hopeless.

Someone in the church told me of a Mormon physician in Columbia, Missouri who could untie my tubes. I had the surgery. It seems like one more act of severing the ties I had with Eric.

Adam misses Eric. He cried for him for so long one day that I finally said, "Let's go find Daddy."

Jeffrey was away at a two week National Guard training camp. I loaded up the children and we set out to find their Daddy.

I told myself that I was doing this for the children, but it may have been because I missed Eric, too. He would often appear in my dreams at the most inopportune times. Randomly, he would step out from behind a tree or something and always say the same thing, "I love you, Shell." And then, he would be gone.

Why anyone with a heart could think they can turn their feelings off and on, is beyond me. I am in such a tangled web!

We did not find Eric that day. I asked him later why he was not seeing the children as much.

"I've been playing ball and working a lot, Shell," was all he said.

He is not the Eric from my dreams, I guess.

October 2, 2010-

> But God commendeth his love toward us,
> In that, while we were yet sinners,
> Christ died for us.
> --Romans 5:8

I wanted my son Adam's funeral to be a time to celebrate his life. But I also wished for it to be a time for each person present to reflect on their own life. Could it be through Adam's death that another soul might be saved?

That's why I wanted Pastor John to read to them about the night my son found the Lord.

74

"One night Adam's mother got the call every Christian mother dreams of receiving. It was Adam, crying and telling her how he had come to know the Lord, confessed his sins, asked forgiveness and became sealed as a child of God."

"He had been watching a video with the Bevier Baptist youth group. When the leader, Denice Dalrymple, was putting it away, a voice came from the back of the room. It was Adam, who said, 'I wanna get saved.' She was able to share with him the most important choice of his life!"

"Adam went out into the world and did amazing things with his life. His friends know him as a fighter (thanks to the Smith genes he carried), and a true friend to others. He did become a great leader. A call to his mother from Afghanistan, after his death, assured her that he had walked straight, never wavered, giving his life for others. Adam truly soared higher than she could have ever dreamed. He will ALWAYS be missed by those whose lives he touched."

"The Lord giveth and the Lord taketh away. Blessed be the name of the Lord."

October 27, 1988-

> When I was a child, I spake as a child,
> I understood as a child, I thought as a child:
> But when I became a man, I put away childish things.
> --1 Corinthians 13:11

We were not able to stay on our farm. We could never get the water pump to work even though we bought a new one. I was at the point of drawing water from the cistern just to cook or wash the babies. The chimney was never rebuilt. Winter would be coming upon us. And, try as I might, I could not acquire a taste for goat's milk!

All in all, we could not afford the cost of living so far out in the country on just one income. But the church teaches mothers to stay home and raise their children. I was torn!

Jeffrey began to stay away from us more and more. He took up bowling again once a week and said he considered staying in town to work out at a gym twice a week too. We did not mind.

Then Jeffrey came up with the idea of joining the Army full time. I pictured the children and I remaining on the farm, but it did not work out. Instead, Carol let us stay in a small house she owned in Moberly until Jeffrey joined.

I tried to make the new house a home for the children. I had lived in some rough houses with Eric, so the plan was to always leave a place better than you found it.

I enrolled Amber and Audrey into a local public school. The boys and I missed them so very much during the day.

The weather outside was cool, yet sunny. Halloween was only a few days away. Adam and Andy and I spent the day decorating the house. I drew pumpkins on paper and had the boys color them. Andy colored a beautiful blue pumpkin and then totally destroyed it trying to cut it out. It didn't matter. I hung what was left of his pumpkin on the window. He was pleased.

Adam was worried that he would not know how to tie his shoes by the time he went to school.

"Here, Buddy, let's practice."

His lesson took up quite a bit of time. Soon it was time to pick up the girls from school. We walked to get them. When I stepped into the gym where the girls were waiting with other town kids, they both flew at me at high speed. We all hugged laughing.

The principal walked over to us smiling. "I wish all the kids could be greeted so warmly."

I wasn't sure what he meant. I just knew that by the end of the day I was about to burst with missing my children, and the feelings were mutual.

When we arrived home, we snacked on apples and peanut butter and played freeze tag outside. Afterward, we laid on a blanket in our yard and I read a Sesame Street story to them. I finished with some Little House in the Big Woods by Laura Ingalls Wilder. The children seemed happy.

As I wrote in my journal that night, I thought how I would have loved just one sunny day like this spent with my own mother. I realized that the children and I could actually be happy anywhere, as long as we had each other.

October 2, 2010-

> Thou tellest my wanderings:
> Put thou my tears into thy bottle:
> Are they not in thy book?
> --Psalm 56:8

Pastor John sat down. Once again, Pastor Scott stood to speak.

This time he was able to continue. He gave a special "thank you" to those leaders who were present, recognizing representatives from almost all the branches of the military.

He mentioned that Governor Nixon had paid a visit the night before and that the government entities were flying their flags at half mast in honor of Adam's sacrifice. He said that Adam would have been so amazed at the turn-out.

The Patriot Guard was given a special thank you from Pastor Scott for all that they do.

"To the Patriot Guard, thank you for standing guard over Adam. At a horrible time, you make a wonderful gesture for all the families who have suffered this great loss. May God bless you for this act of kindness."

It wasn't until Pastor Scott began to speak to the SEALs that his voice cracked a few times.

"But mostly, to the Navy SEALs, HOO-RAH, Adam found a home with you. Adam was born to be a SEAL. He found his place in life with you. You are his brothers in arms. You meant so much to him. I thank you for being here."

He went on to thank the United States Military for the great expense of bringing all these sailors here.

"It's just incredible. Many of you know Vietnam Veterans, and we didn't used to do this. I'm proud of our country for the support."

"So, everyone's presence here means so much, but especially the SEALs. For this has turned a heart break into a majestic occasion."

Pastor Scott then asked the Lord to grant the sailors an extra measure of protection and prayed for victory and success in their missions. He thanked them for their commitment and service to our country. He stated that Adam now joins a long list of sailors who have given their

77

lives so that all of us can enjoy the rights and privileges we have in this country.

"This is a harsh reminder," he continued, "that the price of freedom comes at a terrible cost. But I really believe that if Adam had known that becoming a Navy SEAL would cost his life, he would have done it anyway. He loved being a SEAL."

Pastor Scott shared that he had watched a documentary on TV about the training of Navy SEALs. (I had always avoided that type of information.) In one of the training exercises, SEALs were left out in the ocean all night and had to survive the cold and dangers there. He had asked Adam how that was for him. Adam told him that your body starts to shake and you can't stop it. He had wanted to quit but made up his mind, he was going to do it even if it killed him.

"Now that's a Navy SEAL!" said Pastor Scott.

Then Pastor John read from the Bible in 2 Samuel. Pastor Scott continued, talking about the many warriors found in the Bible. He recalled the way David, as a shepherd boy, had killed Goliath. He asked if anyone knew that Goliath had four brothers. One of his brothers was killed by Jonathan, David's brother in heart. The strongest warriors who fought for David were called the Mighty Men. Jonathan was one of them.They went out on many missions.

"Well, this story, (in 2 Samuel), is about one of those 'excursions.' The men were hiding in a cave from their enemies. They were a small band of warriors. And David makes an off-hand remark, 'I'm thirsty.' Three of the men broke through enemy lines, without regard for their own lives and safety, to get some water for their leader. David was so moved by their actions that he could not bring himself to drink the water. He said, it was like their own life-blood. Instead, he poured it out as a sacrificial offering unto the Lord."

Pastor Scott spoke softly, "Most of us cannot understand that kind of commitment to a cause."

August 28, 1989-

Oh Lord, thou hast searched me, and known me.
Thou knowest my downsitting and mine uprising,
thou understandest my thought afar off.
Thou compassest my path and my lying down,
And art acquainted with all my ways.
--Psalm 139:1-3

Adam, my first-born son, will go to kindergarten this year. What shall I do about him? He has become so distant from me since Eric and I broke up, especially since Jeffrey and I have married. What have I done to that little heart? He seems so full of anger and not the same little boy. I realize now, from college and experience, that my divorce and remarriage was very traumatic for the children. No one told me. Now I have to repair the damage I have done and help these babies be happy again.

I have a BIG problem, however. I do not feel for Jeffrey the way I felt for Eric. Now what? I tried to tell him but he just got angry and clammed up.

Valarie got me an appointment to see a counselor. He was a Mormon counselor, of course. Even so, he was shocked and surprised at all the wrong advice I had been given from church members.

"It takes at least two years to mourn the death of a marriage," he informed me.

Strangely, this knowledge somehow brought relief for me. I wasn't going crazy! I decided to go and see my bishop. Surely he would advise me to separate from Jeffrey after hearing what the counselor had said.

"You're talking about a temple marriage," I was informed by my bishop. "That's not like your marriage to Eric. This one sealed you together for time and all eternity. No, I hate to say it, but you made your bed..."

He was right. How could I even contemplate another divorce? Two wrongs won't bring Eric back! The children will be better off if I just make the best of a bad situation.

Besides, after eight months of trying, I was expecting baby number five!

October 2, 2010-

For God so loved the world,
that he gave his only begotten Son,
That whosoever believeth in him should not perish,
But have everlasting life.
--John 3:16

The funeral for my son was drawing to an end. I sat there stupefied at all that had taken place that day. I looked up at the casket again, knowing that soon it would be lowered into the dark cold earth.

"Oh Adam," I thought. "Could this all be real?" I closed my eyes. A final prayer was being said.

"Someone wake me up from this nightmare! My God, where are You? Take this cup from me! Or take me out of this life right now!"

I opened my eyes to see that the men on the stage were all filing down the stairs to leave. I watched these brave soldiers and sailors. As they walked past my family, they either shook hands with my son, Andy, or gently pounded a fist on Adam's coffin.

--I realized that some of these warriors might not return home from their next mission. Suddenly I could remain seated no longer! I stood at attention for them all. I didn't care if I was the only person in the room standing. I respected those men so much for their service to our country and their friendship to my sons.

The pallbearers took their places around Adam. As they lifted him up, his whole short life flashed before my eyes. So many times he should have been carried on everyone's shoulders: all the ball games he made a difference in, all the friends he went to battle for at home, all the encouragement he provided for others. He was always a hero!

Together we walked outside into the golden sunlight toward the waiting hearse.

October 5, 1989-

I took Adam out of Kindergarten yesterday. He was just
too bored with their silly exercises and such. Every day
he comes home and rolls his eyes and says something like,
"We're on M's today, Mom." Then he stomps off annoyed.

The teacher said she didn't blame me. She knew he was
bored and that he already knew all she was going to teach
this year.

What a personality he has! He has discovered dinosaurs!
We read a book about fossils and he fell in love. It is
funny when someone asks him what he wants to be when
he grows up and he says, "A paleontologist." Most adults
don't even know what that is. He can pronounce it too!
Now he can name several classes of dinosaurs and tell if
they are meat eaters or plant eaters.

He will be so excited in a few days. I'm having a
"dinosaur party" for him. When his friends arrive they
will each make their own dinosaur hat and then play some
dinosaur games and eat cake with dinosaur sprinkles on it.
It will be great.

We are now living on Monroe Street in Moberly. Carol
needed her house so we had to move. Jeffrey never did
get into the Army, something about too many dependants.
Anyway, it's a nice little house in a better neighborhood
and the children like it.

I've decided to have this baby at home. My pregnancy
and delivery with Andy was so very short and uneventful
that I believe it will be fine. I've located two midwives
from Columbia who will take me as a, so called, high risk
delivery. Besides, we cannot afford a hospital delivery.

October 2, 2010-

> Owe no man any thing, but to love one another:
> For he that loveth another hath fulfilled the law.
> --Romans 13:8

The five mile drive from the church to the cemetery was most amazing. My James drove our white van with several of my children and I riding along. The Patriot Guard rode in front and behind the procession. We felt surrounded and safe.

Police, Fire, Rescue Squad, Ambulance, First Responders, and other emergency departments sent vehicles to escort this parade of pain as we made our way west.

Andy had made only one request of us this entire week. "Mom, don't bury Adam at the veteran's cemetery in Jacksonville. He wouldn't want that."

That was exactly what I had planned to do. It is a well kept place to be laid to rest as a hero and an honor to be there. But, after listening to my precious heartbroken son, I reconsidered. We decided that Adam should rest in Bevier, right next to the Grandfather whom he was named after, his Great Grandpa Blackorby. It all fell into place and was the right place for him.

It took a good portion of an hour for everyone to complete the trek to Bevier. All along the way were true patriots with flags and tears for our fallen hero. I recognized many people from Adam's past. Former classmates, friends, teachers, coworkers, and acquaintances all stood along the streets and highway as he took his last car ride.

I saw a group of young Boy Scouts standing at attention with flags held high. I cried as it reminded me of the trips to Columbia I made when Adam became interested in joining the Scouts. He needed hats and shirts and different colored scarves for each rank. He was so handsome in his uniform and took each badge and patch seriously as he earned them. Together we learned the Cub Scout oath and promises. I became a den leader just to keep up with him. His final accomplishment was the coveted Arrow of Light. That seemed to appease him and, after that, he devoted his time to playing basketball and baseball.

I looked to the left in time to see my husband's office as we passed. There stood dear friends where I once stood. I was a different person before, feeling so helpless and sorry for the mother of a fallen soldier. I had shuddered at the thought of following a hearse myself.

I held my hand up to the glass to tell everyone that we were grateful for their sincere grief for us and for their love for my son.

Half way there we drove beneath an overpass. Standing above us were many more people. They held a banner in honor of Adam. They waved to us sadly as we passed.

As we turned into Bevier, the Bevier Fire Department volunteers were saluting us as many of the townspeople watched. Yellow ribbons were tied around every sign and pole along the road. When we pulled into the cemetery, I was told to remain in the van until time to carry Adam to his allotted ground. The wind was cool and I was not dressed warmly.

As I sat there, many of my ambulance coworkers in uniform began to pass by my van. I again put my hand up to the glass and soon each one was reaching out and touching the window to show their love for me. Of all the situations we had endured together, this was truly the most difficult.

I will always cherish that moment. This was MY brotherhood.

June 8, 1990-

And great earthquakes shall be in divers places,
And famines, and pestilences;
And fearful sights and great signs
shall there be from heaven.
--Luke 21:11

A major earthquake was predicted for Missouri today. For months it has been the topic of conversation. It is about 9:30 PM and so far nothing has happened. Am I possibly disappointed?

I have been so worried about it. There have been several small earthquakes lately as well as tornadoes and floods. Why not be ready to face any disaster? I took a class on earthquake preparedness and made little blue jean backpacks for the children to grab if we had to evacuate our home. I had even screwed book cases to the walls to keep them from injuring the children if they should fall. I have just about frightened the children to death with it all. Especially Adam who notices everything I do and worries about us.

What a sensitive young man. I can't even watch any shows about unsolved mysteries in front of Adam. He ponders the fact that family members could vanish or killers could never be caught and tells me about it weeks later. He is not fidgety or nervous, just watchful and mindful of others.

At least if there had been an earthquake, we would have been ready!

October 2, 2010-

> The eyes of the Lord are upon the righteous,
> And his ears are open unto their cry.
> --Psalm 34:15

Kyle opened my van door and offered his arm. I followed as my son was carried to his grave. His casket was gently placed atop a temporary pedestal. The funeral flowers had been brought from Macon and lovingly stacked around the casket, obliterating the dark hole beneath him. Yet, I knew it was there. I've always loved the earth and the feel of its soil in my hands, but at that moment, I truly hated the thought of it. It seemed to be hungrily waiting there to swallow my Adam forever.

A tent had been set up to shelter our family from the wind. Once seated, it dawned on me that, although a tarp and boards had been placed beneath us, we were actually stepping on Grandpa Blackorby's grave. I felt disrespectful. Then I remembered how very excited he was when we asked him all those years ago if we could name Adam after him. That memory somehow made me feel as if Grandpa would be forgiving of our intrusion.

"My children!" I screamed in my heart as they slowly

trudged in around me. "Oh, how I've neglected every one of you this week!"

I should have been the strong mother they knew. I should have held them and reassured them that we would get through this. Yet, I felt helpless, as if some unseen force held me captive. I could not move toward them and could only look in pity, knowing we were all hostages of grief.

I looked down to see that someone had laid a fuzzy red blanket across my lap. The warmth of it surprised me as I realized that I had been cold. I appreciated that small act of kindness.

There we sat for the longest time, as people continued to arrive at the cemetery, park and walk to where we were. I did not mind the wait. I wanted to tell someone that my Adam had once been afraid of the dark. I didn't think it would be a good idea to put him down there.

"Wait a minute," I thought to myself, "he is not here!"

There is a tomb in Israel that many believe is the one owned by Joseph of Arimathea. He once loaned it for a weekend to Jesus. When you enter you see a plaque on the door which reads, 'HE IS NOT HERE—FOR HE IS RISEN.'

"Adam is not here!" I reminded myself, "He is with the Lord!"

July 8, 1991-

And He took a child, and set him in the midst of them:
And when He had taken him in his arms, He said to them,
Whosoever shall receive one of such children
in my name, receiveth me:
And whosoever shall receive me, receiveth not me,
but Him that sent Me.
--Mark 9:36-37

So much has happened since I've written in my journal! I did not have my fifth baby at home. When I was due, I saw the midwives for the last time. I was having complications. They panicked and told me to go to the hospital, and then they left. It turned out to be pre-eclampsia, and I had a miserable delivery.

Never just show up at a hospital when you have only been seeing midwives throughout your entire pregnancy. To the hospital staff, it is as if you've had NO prenatal care. They just about don't like you. The good result from this bad situation was that I safely delivered my beautiful baby, Abigail Rose! She is adorable.

Once, when Abbie was only about five months old, the children and I had just returned home from grocery shopping. I had so many bags of food to carry in and was exhausted. When Adam begged to carry her into the house for me, I went against my better judgment and allowed it. I went on inside and began to put things away in the kitchen. Suddenly, I heard Abbie screaming! As I rushed onto the back porch I saw Adam hurrying inside with her.

"What happened?" I yelled.

"I don't know, she just started screaming," was his concerned reply.

"This baby is hurt!"

But, after checking Abbie out and finding no marks whatsoever on her, I apologized to him for getting so upset. He went into the other room for a few minutes then returned to me.

"Mom, I have something to tell you," he explained quietly. "When I was carrying Abbie into the house, I accidently dropped her."

"Buddy, you said you didn't know what happened to her," I tried to stay calm.

"I lied 'cause I thought you'd be mad at me."

"Well, you've got that right. But the reason I'm the most upset is because you lied to me. What if she had needed to go to the hospital and you kept it from me?"

I did punish Adam that day for lying, but I witnessed a change in him. It had really bothered him that he had not told the truth. He is growing up!

There are other changes and additions in our lives now too. One year and one month after I had Abigail, I gave birth to Alaina Grace. Hers was an even more frightening delivery, as she was my first emergency cesarean. Chopping and carrying in wood from outside may have had something to do with the problems of that birth, but who can tell me what's right or wrong?

We have moved back to Macon. We are living in

Valarie's house again. The same house the children and I ran to when we left Eric. It seems like a lifetime ago.

Oh yes, and I'm going to have another baby in the fall for Adam to carry into the house!

October 2, 2010-

> Jesus said unto him, if thou canst believe,
> all things are possible to him that believeth.
> And straightway the father of the child cried out,
> and said with tears,
> Lord, I believe; help thou mine unbelief.
> --Mark 9:23-24

In the distance, I could hear the last of the Patriot Guards as they entered the cemetery. The motors of their massive bikes became silent and a hush fell over all those gathered there.

As I glanced over at T-Roy, I felt so very sorry for him. He and Adam had recently gone on a cruise together with their girlfriends. They were all so close.

Pastor Scott was given the sign to begin. He walked in front of our family.

"I'd like to begin this committal service with the praying of the Lord's Prayer." The wind blowing through the trees caused the multitude of flags to snap to and fro. "Would you pray this prayer with me? Our Father…"

"…Thy kingdom come…" I almost choked as I recited these words.

"Come now oh Lord!" I suggested to the Inventor of Time. This would be a perfect moment to make His grand return!

He chose not to come. Adam was still gone. I remained seated and Pastor Scott continued.

"In Micah four, it says, 'But in the last days it shall come to pass, that the mountain of the house of the Lord shall be established in the top of the mountains, and it shall be exalted above the hills; and the people shall flow unto it.

"And many nations shall come, and say, come, and let us go up to the mountain of the Lord, and to the house of the God of Jacob; and he will teach us of his ways, and we will walk in his paths: for the law shall go forth of Zion, and the word of the Lord from Jerusalem.

"And he shall judge among many people, and rebuke strong nations afar off; and they shall beat their swords into plowshares, and their spears into pruning hooks: nation shall not lift up a sword against nation, neither shall they learn war anymore." (Micah 4:1-3).

The weight of these words sank into my heart. I wished we were at a time of peace already.

Pastor Scott seemed to read my thoughts.

"In the New Testament, Jesus is quoted as saying, 'Until the end, there shall be wars and rumors of wars. (Mark 13:7) And, because of wars, all nations, OUR nation, has to have soldiers that fight, and even die for us, like Adam.

"When Adam first said that he was going to join the Navy, and become a Navy SEAL, there were doubters. And even in this past week I've had, I don't know how many people, come to me and say, 'I didn't think Adam could do it.' I knew that if Adam ever really got the chance to go through SEAL training, he was such a good athlete that, physically, he could do it.

"There were other people that didn't think that Adam could take the discipline of the military-- because of Adam. (Some chuckles were heard from those who knew Adam best. They probably remembered how Adam despised authority.) They felt that the military would keep pushing him, and sooner or later he would slug somebody, end up in Leavenworth, or get kicked out of the service. (Again, knowing snickers could be heard from the huddled crowd.) I think he did some of that anyway. But they liked him because he was good at his job.

"I told him I didn't have any doubts about his abilities, his determination and drive, his willingness to fight and even to suffer. But, I didn't quite believe he would ever let them cut that long, wavy, blond hair! You didn't mess with Adam's hair! (Now, everyone burst out in laughter, amid their tears. Adam was known for his shaggy, sun bleached hair.)

"But he did let them cut it. And, he did make it. And he has done us proud! I'm very proud today of him. And, I'm proud to be an American.

"This doesn't take away from the loss of Adam. But, it

sure helps. God bless you for being here. Thank you.

"We've come to the time where we must lay Adam's earthly body down to his final resting place." Pastor Scott was wrapping up his message.

"Oh, no," I screamed to myself. Don't you dare touch my son!"

"But the Adam that I knew and loved…" Pastor Scott made a motion towards the hill of flowers where my baby rested. "…the real Adam-- his spirit, his soul-- is not here."

I was ashamed at how quickly I had forgotten this fact.

"According to the Word of God, by faith, he is now in the presence of his Heavenly Father. And by that, and through my tears and your loss and our hurt, we can think of him as being with God in Heaven. And that brings us happiness and joy, even though now we must walk through this valley. Let us pray."

Pastor Scott prayed then. He thanked God for all those who came and showed support to our family. He said it brought comfort. Then he recognized the Great Comforter that comes only from the Lord, His Spirit.

"We pray the peace of God upon all that knew and loved Adam. And now Lord, we just release into Your care, his spirit. We know that You take care of him even now. We pray these things in Jesus name. Amen."

August 31, 1992-

> Confess your faults one to another,
> and pray one for another, that ye may be healed.
> The effectual fervent prayer of a righteous man
> availeth much.
> --James 5:16

I had thought to home school all of my children, but I keep having more babies. Adam will be going to third grade this year. He is very quick to learn and even though he says he hates school, I can see he is learning and even enjoying some things.

Jeffrey and I were separated for about four months. He can do whatever he wants to me, but you don't mess with my babies! I was just fine with living apart but the Stake

President of the Church told me that "the Lord wants (me) to work out (my) marriage."

I took Jeffrey back but will never trust or respect him again.

If it weren't for the temple marriage, I would have been gone a long time ago. Sometimes I wonder just how important that marriage for time and all eternity is to me. I do know that my marriage to him will guarantee that my kids can reach the Celestial Kingdom. Here's to living as a martyr.

I've bought a new journal so I will finish up this one with some of the poems I've written about the children.

My Son
He wants to know about the world,
And explore it's every part.
He yearns to sample all he sees,
With his innocent, growing heart.
So how can I tell him he is too young?
And that he must walk before he can run?

He has a sense of right and wrong,
Which good men tend to seek.
If he can keep it for very long,
Then he can help the weak.
To make their way on a troubled Earth,
And they'll praise the day that I gave birth!
To Adam

From Mother
Could I but leave you these words of hope?
Should you ever feel at the end of your rope?
Don't make it this world that you try to please.
And know you are never taller than when on your knees.
To My Children

Precious Thoughts
Tiny handprints upon my back,
The remains of a chocolate hug,
I hate to launder them away,
These emblems of innocent love.

Happy Day!
Happy day, happy day,
When Mommy says "go out and play,"
But happier is my happy day,
When Mommy says "LET'S go and play!"

Stalling
I can't go to sleep till you sing me a song.
I won't make a peep if you make it last long!
To Adam

At the Playground
There's crawling and climbing
And calling to Mom,
"Can you please push me high in this swing?"
The laughter that seems to float by in the breeze,
Such long lasting memories bring.

October 2, 2010-

In the sweat of thy face shalt thou eat bread,
Till thou return unto the ground;
for out of it wast thou taken:
For dust thou art, and unto dust shalt thou return.
--Genesis 3:19

"Honor Guard," came a shout from somewhere outside the tent, "ten-hut!"

I could hear movement, but did not try to see what it was. I did notice that the pallbearers all turned to face each other.

Before I could prepare myself, a SEAL began to play taps. It was a haunting and lonely sound. All around us those in uniform saluted.

Several SEALs moved toward Adam's casket and removed the flag that draped the top. They carried it to the pallbearers and together, with professional ceremony, folded it. I remembered that it would be handed to me.

"How can I take this flag?" I wondered. "This material has just come from the top of my son's casket!"

Time seemed to slow down. When the gentlemen with

the flag finally stood in front of me, I could see my arms reach out and take it. Oh, how very different this moment was from when these same arms reached out for the first time and took a crying, blue, hungry baby boy into them. I hugged the flag to my chest.

Kyle stepped forward and removed several potted plants from the edge of the dark abyss where my son would soon be lowered. I thought this very odd.

One by one the Navy SEALs, starting with Jack, removed their trident pins from off their uniforms and began to file past the newly made hole. As Jack approached it, he kissed his pin and dropped it down inside Adam's vault hitting the floor with a metallic clank. We could hear the sound over and over as each friend walked solemnly by. Their tiny tokens of love will forever rest beneath my boy.

December 9, 1992-

Even a child is known by his doings,
Whether his work be pure, and whether it be right.
--Proverbs 20:11

Baby Anna Kay has arrived! She was born on November 12. Will I have any more children? No way! I promised myself I would quit when I turned thirty and that was a week ago. Whew, I'm glad that part is over. Now I can settle down and raise the seven children I have.

Today there is snow covering our world outside. Adam and Andy wanted to go out after school and build a snowman. I thought Abbie would like to watch from the window. They are having such a good time!

Adam must always outdo himself in everything he does. He won't be happy with a pansy little snowman. He is insisting on a huge, three boulder sized giant!

I couldn't stand the thought that Abbie must always watch from the window so I have suited her up in layers of clothing and she is right out there helping. She is walking across the yard for a tiny handful of snow and then all the way back, just to pat it into the boys' Goliath. So cute!

It is wonderful to have my little "chicks" living close

92

to me. I hope these are the last days so I can be here with them, protecting them. The world can fall apart around us as long as we have each other!

We are struggling all the time to buy food and pay bills, yet I believe we are the wealthiest 'poor' people in the world! There is a small country in eastern Africa called Somalia where thousands of people are starving right now. The UN has sent food and supplies to them but someone in power there is intercepting it. We are sending troops to help. I'm glad. It is called Operation Restore Hope. I'm proud of our men.

If these aren't the last days, I want my sons to grow up and become protectors, too. I have become a den leader for the Cub Scouts just so Adam will be active in it. He is so handsome in his uniform! He was upset the first time I made him wear it to school but I want the boys to wear them on meeting days so the other children will see they are involved and have respect for them. He doesn't mind now.

I have also insisted that Adam speak more at church. We had a program in which he had a very big part. He did not want me to help him memorize his lines. I worried that he would get up in front of all those people and freeze. He did excellent!

Will he always have such an 'over the top' personality?

October 2, 2010-

> To everything there is a season,
> and a time to every purpose under heaven:
> A time to be born, and a time to die;
> A time to love, and a time to hate;
> A time of war, and a time of peace.
> > --Ecclesiastes 3:1,2a &8

After the SEALs filed past Adam and said their good-byes, they went out into the yard and stood at attention.

Two representatives from the Patriot Guard came to stand in front of us. One was a man and the other, a woman. The woman knelt down in front of me.

"We just want to thank you for inviting us to ride for your son today. We have a plaque to present to you and I'd like to read it to you if that's OK." I agreed.

On Behalf of a Grateful America
And the
Patriot Guard Riders
Please Accept Our Sincere
Condolences on Your Tragic Loss.
May Your Pain be Tempered
By the Knowledge that

SO2 Adam Olin Smith
US Navy SEAL
Operation Enduring Freedom/Afghanistan
Is a
True American Hero

Patriot Guard Riders
"Standing for Those Who Stood for Us"

"Thank you so much for all you've done for us," I said softly.

"It's been our pleasure," she told me.

With that, they stepped aside. Several of the SEALs came by to shake our hands and hug us. Then the remaining crowd consoled our pain with kind words.

James had reserved the Round House in Macon. It is a round, cabin-like reception hall that sits at the edge of a lake. We wanted to have some time with the SEALs and the girls before they had to leave for the airport at St. Louis. My husband and Eric had ordered several pizzas and treats delivered there.

Once everyone had spoken to us and, either left the cemetery, or were gathering into groups, my husband leaned over and said, "We should probably head over to Macon to the Round House. There may be people there already."

I felt panic rush into my heart. I had thought to stay there as they lowered my Adam into the ground. He still lay in front of us at the top of his mountain of flowers. How cruel would that be to go to a "party" and just leave him with strangers?

"I was thinking I would just stay here for awhile," I said

94

with a shaky voice. "It's not finished yet."

"Are you sure you want to do that?"

"Yes."

"Then I will stay until you are ready."

"Honey, I can't leave yet!" I said with unwarranted alarm in my voice.

Why was I so worried? He said he would wait with me. What exactly was I trying to accomplish? It wasn't that I needed "closure." It was the mother in me, needing somehow to perform one last act of protection. My baby was going to be forced against his will into a dark hole!

"God, help them to understand what I'm feeling!"

It did not happen. I felt the responsibility of taking care of everyone else come over me, and I relinquished.

Maybe that was God's answer. ONCE AGAIN, He gave me peace in my heart, that HE was the One taking care of my Adam.

I left for the Round House.

March 2, 1993-

Children, obey your parents in the Lord: for this is right.
Honour thy father and mother;
which is the first commandment with promise;
That it may be well with thee,
and thou mayest live long on the earth.
--Ephesians 6:1-3

What will these boys do next? They are like two bear cubs. Why do my boys fight ALL the time? It is about to drive me crazy! If I use anger, they fear me. If I use lectures, they get bored. Even if I use tears, it doesn't seem to affect them. What is the answer?

Last night, at bath time, Adam and Andy were pushing and shoving each other. That's not such a big deal, except that their bathroom is on the second floor. Andy shoved Adam so hard that he was pushed into the window! It broke and Adam began to fall out backwards.

Andy panicked. He reached out just in time to grab Adam, pulling him back inside! The result was a wicked looking cut to Andy's wrist. I had a panic attack over that upstairs window's location, so low to the floor. I moved a hamper in front of it after that close call.

The incident reminded me of the way that I felt one day when Adam was a baby, just beginning to walk. I was in the basement at Grandma Blackorby's house doing laundry. I thought I had shut the door at the top of the stairs, so I was surprised, a few moments later, when I heard the door open. I saw what I thought was a rag doll, rolling down the wooden steps. It was perfectly silent.

About half way down, just before the object fell off the edge of the stairs, I realized in horror that it was my baby Adam! He landed in the center of a large box of canning jars! I was frozen, fearful of what I would find.

When I got to the child, who was screaming by now, there was not one mark on Adam! And, not one jar was broken! What a miracle boy he is!

These boys have me near the end of my sanity! I pray that the rest of my children will be girls after this.

October 2, 2010-

> Glory to God in the highest,
> And on earth peace,
> Good will toward men.
> --Luke 2:14

Our gathering at the Round House was actually a relaxed time of fellowship. As I looked around at Adam's many friends, I felt such love for each of them.

These were his fellow warriors. I knew that they were bonded as brothers forever. I had no idea what dangers they had faced together. And probably would not want to know.

All too soon our time together came to a close. Several of the girls had reserved a hotel near the St. Louis airport. They needed to head that way as it began to grow dark. The SEALs had come from both coasts of our nation. Now they had to return to their responsibilities. I cried as they departed.

Charlotte asked if I would fly out to Virginia in a few days to attend a memorial service for the fallen SEALs who had died with Adam in the chopper accident. I wanted to

Michele and her children--

    Back: Audrey, Adam, Andy, Amber, Allie, Angel

    Center: Austen, Michele

    Front: Abbie, Anna

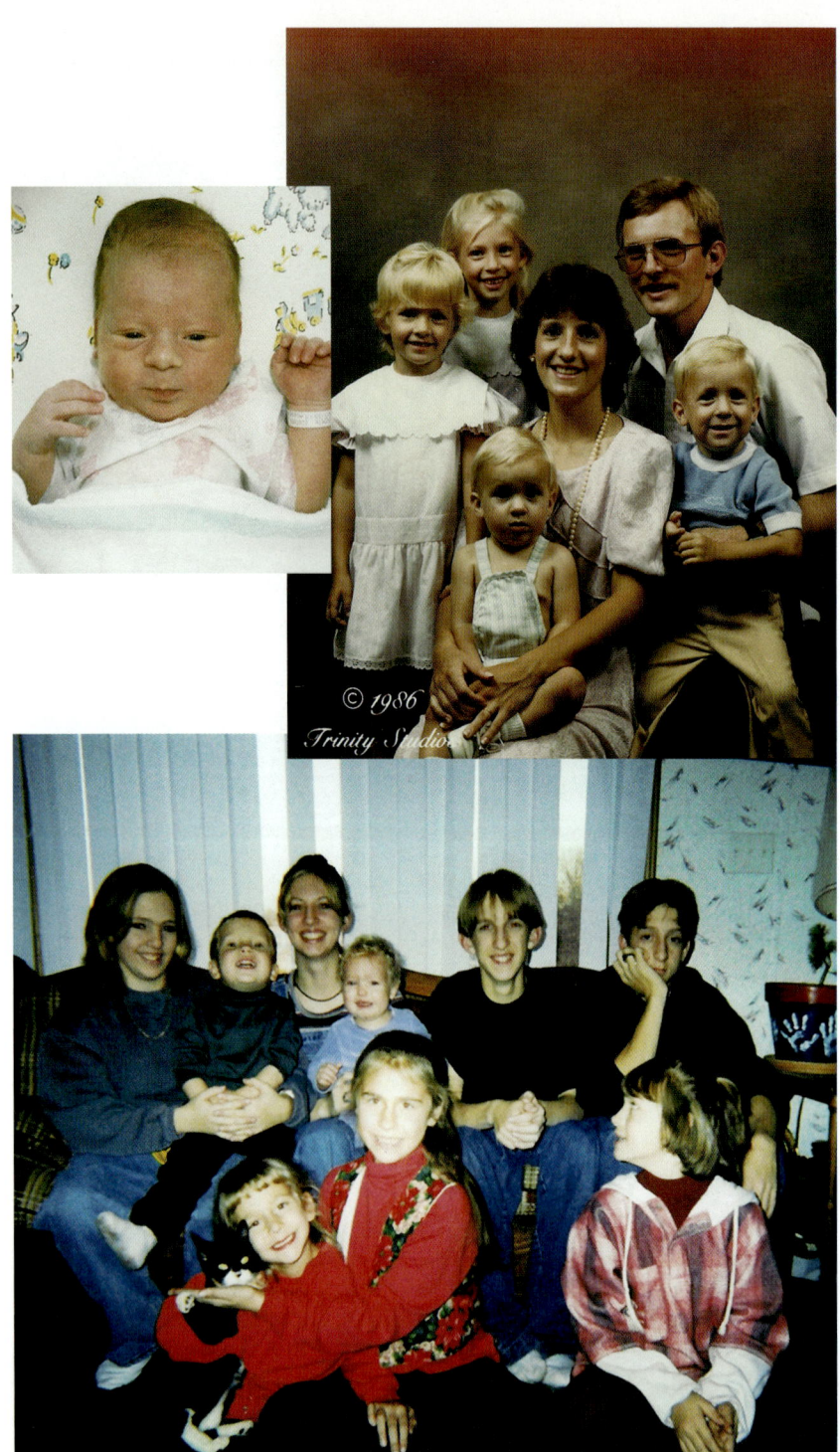

go home to my room and lock myself inside until I died. Instead, I promised her I would bring the children and attend the service.

When everyone was gone, and it was finally time for me to go home, I had the urge to rush back to the cemetery and check on Adam. My husband convincd me that I was exhausted, and needed to rest.

Why is he so practical?

March 16, 1994-

And why beholdest thou the mote
that is in thy brother's eye,
But considerest not the beam that is in thine own eye?
--Matthew 7:3

We've moved once again. This time we are buying a small hobby farm on the edge of Excello, Missouri. We have a bit of land, a big red barn, some animals and freedom! I love it here.

I bought myself a scroll saw for Christmas to make rocking chairs for the three younger girls. Adam realized I could fashion swords and shields with this saw.

"Look what my mom made!" I overheard him tell a neighbor boy. "I'll see if she will make you one too!" I almost passed out. Am I raising little warriors? Maybe I am the reason my boys fight too much. Now I'm supplying them with weapons!

The boys are doing well in Cub Scouts. I should have taken pictures of all the pinewood derby cars and even the soap box car I helped the boys build!

Adam is about to receive his Arrow of Light award. This is the highest award he can get in the program. He worked hard for it. I love to see the patriotism they are developing!

In my spare time for the last several years, I have attended CPR and First Aid classes to be better prepared for emergencies with all the children. I read in the paper several months ago about E.M.T. training through the adult education classes offered in Macon.

"Emergency Medical Technician class. Maybe that will

give me more advanced skills to deal with accidents." I signed up.

"Wait till we take the state exam and get licensed," I overheard someone say the first night.

"Oh, I won't be needing that kind of stress," I determined to myself. "I will just learn all I can from the class and politely say goodbye."

Now, months later, I have found a new love in emergency services! I may even take that frightening exam just to see if I can pass! The children love to hear me retell the stories I hear in class. And they really enjoy being my guinea pigs when it comes to practicing bandaging or splinting.

My Mormon church frowned upon my activities. This education could lead to me working outside the home, and even independence! Maybe in a non-conscious way I am preparing for a change in our future. Is that what I want?

It doesn't hurt to have a back up plan.

October 5, 2010-

For God hath not given us the spirit of fear;
But of love, and of power, and of a sound mind.
--2 Timothy 1:7

There has not been much time to ponder our lives since Adam's funeral. For the past three days I have been in and out of doctor's offices and hospitals with my Allie. She is only nineteen and experiencing a severe case of kidney stones. We had hoped she would pass them in time to fly to Virginia for the memorial service, but she hasn't. The doctors feel it would be too much for her. Sadly, I left her with James' daughter, Lindsay. They are close friends. She will be cared for well.

Somehow the rest of the family packed, made it to the airport, and flew with me to the east coast. I'm so numb with grief and exhaustion. It has made me snappy with my family. If I hear any laughter or light heartedness, I ask them to be quiet.

Everyone else is treating us with respect and kindness. We've been driven to a beautiful hotel. Several rooms have been provided for Eric's and my families.

The girls brought Charlotte to visit with us. She seems to want to talk about the good times she had with Adam. I like to hear the stories too. We've spent an evening of getting to know each other and missing my boy.

"Usually there is a representative from each family of the fallen who will say a few words about their hero," Matt stopped by to inform us about the upcoming memorial service. "Do you know of anyone who would speak about Adam?" No one volunteered.

I didn't want my son to be the only one not represented. "I will do it."

Matt looked surprised.

November 8, 1995-

> Now therefore hearken unto me, O ye children:
> For blessed are they that keep my ways.
> Hear instruction, and be wise, and refuse it not.
> --Proverbs 8:32-33

Once again, I am alone with my children. I guess I have been all along but now it is official. I have sent Jeffrey packing because I just could not go on another year the way it was. He didn't even argue. He seemed grateful to be going. It was so sad, I almost felt sorry for him.

My biggest shock was the way the church treated me afterward. I was almost shunned. There was no love-bombing or fellowshipping the way they did when I broke up with Eric. My visiting teachers only came ONE time. They seemed nervous and on edge. I wanted to shout at them as they delivered their canned lesson.

"Hey, it's me! I have served along-side you for years! Don't you recognize me?"

Not one word was mentioned about my status. When they hurried away, I was left standing there holding a potted evergreen tree they gave me.

One day I received a call from my very best friend, Valarie.

"Michele, I feel like I owe you an apology," she said in her quiet way.

99

"What ever for?" I asked.

"I feel like we convinced you to leave Eric and marry Jeffrey."

"It's OK," I lied. "There was a lot wrong with that marriage."

Why couldn't I just say it? "Yes, you did this to me and now you have left me hanging!"

The conversation ended with her saying we should get together soon. I agreed. We both knew it would never be the same between us.

Soon, I was put on church disciplinary probation for not living up to my beliefs as a Mormon. That hurt more than my breakup with Jeffrey.

I received my EMT license in August, 1994, and was hired for ambulance work. At the same time I got a job dispatching for 911.

I love both jobs but am away from home now a lot. I hired a sitter and my mother helps some. Neither are the best for my kids. I get off work at midnight and drive to retrieve sleeping children just to take them home and do the same thing the next day.

Along with missing my children, I have found that I am not on top of their activities as I once was. Several of them, possibly led by Adam, threw rocks through a window and got into trouble. Then Adam began coming home from school with money. When I asked him where he got it, he said he was drawing pictures for different kids. They were paying him, probably with their lunch money! (He is a good artist, I have to admit.) I need to get them more involved in other activities.

"Mom, can I play football?" Adam asked me one day.

I was very apprehensive. "What if you get hurt?"

"Please, Mom?"

Finally, as the usual guilt took over, I said yes. After all, he had been playing summer baseball for several years and was very good at it.

I think he is a natural at any sport he plays. I have to admit, too, I am rather proud of being his mom on the sidelines.

I like his football coach, Pat Quinley. He knew I had some financial difficulties and found a pair of used cleats for Adam. When I asked how much for them he answered,

"Don't worry about it."

He doesn't know who he is saying that to. I worry about everything!

October 6, 2010-

> He healeth the broken in heart,
> and bindeth up their wounds.
> He telleth the number of the stars;
> he calleth them all by their names.
> Great is our Lord, and of great power:
> his understanding is infinite.
> --Psalm 146:3-5

Our drive from the hotel was similar to the trek from the church to the cemetery in Missouri. The motorcade of vans carrying each family was surrounded by the ever faithful Patriot Guard. Our family was so large that we took up several vans.

First we were taken to the Heritage Building for a light breakfast, and then loaded up in the vans again.

After a short ride, we pulled up in front of the building where the memorial would be held.

"Is this the place?"

"Where do we go now?"

"I need to use the bathroom."

As the questions and comments continued from my children, I began to lose patience again.

"Let's just get out and wait until we are told where to enter, OK?"

Again, I wondered why I felt so irritated at those I love the most.

Once we entered the building, we were taken to a section of a hallway that had been temporarily curtained off. We were told that in a few minutes we would each be escorted to the auditorium. This gave us time to pull ourselves together.

"Are you ready?" I looked up into Matt's face as he held out his arm to escort me.

"As ready as I'll ever be, I guess."

As we entered the room the sound of bagpipes keening

almost knocked me down. The sound of their wailing has haunted the clan McPherson, my ancestors, down through the ages. Traditionally, the bagpipes are to be played at all of our funerals. James had done his best to find a player for Adam's funeral but we could not at such a late date. Now the mournful lament surrounded me. My knees felt weak. I tightened my hold on Matt's arm as we walked down the aisle.

The parents of the fallen sailors were taken to the front of the room where large photos of our boys flanked each side of the stage. There was Adam, with his big grin.

We walked slowly by. On the stage we passed four short wooden crosses. Each held our son's uniforms and gear, from the helmet to the boots. I could almost reach out and touch them, and I cried as I realized this was the very clothing and equipment that once covered my Adam when his body was full of life and laughter.

Next to their gear, four glass fronted boxes held each sailor's many medals. Adam had never spoken of his accomplishments. Seeing the tangible evidence of his dangerous missions made me feel more proud of his humility than any object he had earned.

As we were escorted to our seats in the front row, I saw that my children were all right behind me.

A gentleman approached one of two podiums on the stage and ordered the color guard to proceed. They marched out in crisp white uniforms, carrying our beloved flag. The National Anthem played loudly over the speakers. Then, as professionally as they had entered, the color guard marched away.

Standing at the other podium, a chaplain began to speak. "Psalm 46:1 and 2 says, 'God is our refuge and strength; an ever present help in trouble, therefore we will not fear.' Let us pray.

"Holy God we gather here today to honor the lives of Lieutenant Brendan Looney, Senior Chief Criptologic Technician, David McLendon, Special Warfare Operator Second Class, Adam Smith, and Special Warfare Operator Third Class, Denis Miranda.

"Lord, we ask You today to be with us as we remember their lives, their sacrifice, the impact they had on those who knew and worked by their sides. Lord, we set this time aside to honor the lives lost; lives of service and lives of honor. Stand with us Lord as we remember them.

"Most merciful God, whose wisdom is beyond our understanding. We ask You Lord, to pour out Your grace on the families of our brothers as they deal with their grief. Surround them with Your love, Lord, so that they may not be overwhelmed by their loss, but have confidence in Your goodness and in Your strength to meet the days that come.

"We put our trust in You, O Lord. We have confidence in Your grace. Amen."

The chaplain sat down and the announcer welcomed us to the memorial. He also passed the Navy's heartfelt condolences to the families of the fallen from the 101st Airborne Aviation Squad. Many of us had lost loved ones on that dreadful morning.

As the announcer welcomed several distinguished guests, my eyes kept wandering to my son's happy face in his picture. I had not seen that particular picture before and wondered what had just happened to make him smile so big.

It did not take much to bring on his smile.

July 28, 1996-

But if from thence thou shalt seek the Lord thy God,
thou shalt find Him,
If thou seek Him with all thy heart and with all thy soul.
--Deuteronomy 4:29

I have met the most amazing man! While working ambulance one day, we were refueling the truck, when this guy drove up.

"Michele, I want you to meet Connar, my cousin," my partner introduced us.

I was hooked. For weeks I was after my coworker to get us together. It didn't happen. Finally, I wrote Connar a short letter. I reminded him of when we met and told him to stop by the next time he was in Macon to get a soda or something.

"Michele, that guy called again," one of the nurses at work told me a few days after I'd sent the letter. We had been hit hard that day so I was out a lot on the ambulance.

Finally he'd gotten through and we set up our first date. We were going to see the movie Twister.

We have been seeing each other ever since. My children love him and I have to say, I am quite fond of him myself. He owns and operates a fish farm about forty minutes away which he built from nothing. He is a Mizzou graduate with a degree in agricultural engineering. And, he is very charming.

Sometimes I stop and ask myself why I would want to get involved with anyone again. Then I remember all those lonely years being married to Jeffrey. I feel like a rebellious teenager now.

My job does not allow me to get to church as often as I would like. And, when I do go, I only get the silent treatment from some of my best friends. One Sunday I was told that the branch president wanted to see me in his office.

"Michele, I understand that your truck was parked at a certain person's house at 11:00 Saturday night."

This happened before I met Connar. I had been at a friend's house watching movies and our children were there too. I was furious. I demanded that a known busy body be called in to the office, too.

"Are you following me?" I asked as she strolled in and sat down.

"Michele, we do it because we love you."

I had at least expected her to deny her stalking me! I backed down, fumbled for an excuse and wimped out some sort of an explanation. All the time just wanting to escape their judging stares. And yes, I was creeped-out that they would go as far as to follow me.

Even then, I still believed the Mormon Church was true and perfect. The doctrine ran deep inside of me. I may have thrown away a temple marriage, but I held on to my faith.

I could work my way out of this mess.

October 6, 2010-

Prepare the table,
Watch in the watchtower, eat, drink:
Arise, ye princes, and anoint the shield.
--Isaiah 21:5

My thoughts came back to the room when Ed Winter, Commander Naval Special Warfare Command (NSW) was introduced. Thumbing through his notes, he walked to the empty stand.

"Teammates, friends and family, I believe that a handful of courageous men of strong will and character, with the right training, the right experience, the right knowledge, can change the course of history. Or perhaps, preserve the course of history.

"What do I mean by that? Let's imagine that Osama bin Laden had been killed or captured before 9-11.

"9-11 changed our lives, all of our lives forever. Had he been killed or captured before then, things would be the same. It wouldn't be changed. History would have been preserved.

"But why do I say that? Because I will tell you that every day, since 9-11, future bin Ladens have been tracked, pursued, captured or killed around the world. Not only on the battlefields of Iraq or Afghanistan, but in many places that I can't talk about here.

"And the men who pursued them and tracked them, the men who did that, were part of our team. Those were those courageous men that I talked about.

"Yes, a handful of courageous men of strong will and character, the men we lost; Blake, Brendan, Denis, Smity (a nickname for Adam), those were those courageous men.

"Sometimes you have to wonder where those courageous men come from. How did they get to where they were? We trained them. NSW, the battlefields, gave them that experience that I talked about. And the training and experience together; that gave them the knowledge that they needed to do their jobs.

"That was the easy part. The hard part is that strong will and character, that courage.

"Strong will? You guys know what I'm talking about

here. They wouldn't be part of our community if they hadn't possessed strong will.

"Uncompromising character, that's that guy that always does what is right even when nobody is looking.

"Courage? That's going out to face the enemy every night, or running to rescue your team mates that are in trouble, knowing that that could be the end of your own life, yet still going bravely.

"These characteristics, they began in their homes. These men were taught, nurtured and raised by their families.

"These men of great strength and value are the men that we lost on 21 September, 2010; Brendan, Denis, Blake, Smity. They came from the Looney family, the Smith family, the Miranda family, the McLendon family.

"I know these families are all proud. They should be proud for raising such men."

October 18, 1996-

> My son, if thine heart be wise,
> my heart shall rejoice, even mine.
> Yea, my reins shall rejoice,
> when thy lips speak right things.
> --Proverbs 23:15-16

My Adam is becoming a man! We are spending more and more time on the fish farm. He is learning to drive tractors, swim like a fish and even seine ponds. It's hard work, but he seems to love it. He is only thirteen, yet I am already noticing how strong he has become.

"Mom, Mom, Mom?" He came to me one day.

"What, Buddy?" I said a bit annoyed.

Adam had developed a habit that, when he really wanted something, he would approach me and quickly say 'Mom' three times in a row before I could answer! It was irritating! I always knew that, whatever he wanted, he would not take 'no' easily.

"Are you going to marry Connar?"

"I don't know about that one. We've only been dating for six months."

I instantly thought of how I had rushed into two other

106

marriages. Look how those turned out. My track record with relationships leaves a lot to be desired. But he is so handsome, and talented and fun! And my kids all love him!

"I think you should. Then we could be on the fish farm all the time," Adam snapped me back to reality.

"We'll see, now let's talk about this progress report."

Adam's grades had suddenly begun to drop and I, of course, was worried.

"Isn't that a sign of drug use? He never had a problem maintaining A's before. He is also more moody than usual these days..." My over active imagination began to run away from me.

"Mom, school is boring. Can we go to Connar' this weekend?"

I'd gotten my answer.

October 6, 2010-

So that we may boldly say,
The Lord is my helper,
And I will not fear what man shall do unto me.
--Hebrews 13:6

Commander Winter could only imagine how proud I was of Adam.

"To these families, thank you. I am grateful to all of you for raising such men, and for giving us your sons, your grandsons, your brothers. For making them a part of our brotherhood. We will always remember them.

"To the Force, our enemies are smarter, more clever and more dangerous than ever. However, you are better than we have ever been. Frankly, I couldn't compete with you guys with what I was thirty years ago. You are better. You are stronger, faster, and smarter. You are multitask-able problem solvers. You're not just warriors.

"The nation demands more from you than ever. I know many guys out there who have made a dozen deployments. Either Iraq, Afghanistan, or again, those places that I can't talk about. But the most important thing about you is that you are all true patriots.

"Most of you are new to the teams since 9/11. You

signed up because your country had been attacked. Because your families, your neighbors, your communities, your way of life was threatened. You did this knowing that very soon you would step onto the battlefield and risk your own life.

"SEAL Ethos says, 'In times of war or uncertainty there is a special breed of warrior ready to answer our Nation's call. A common man with uncommon desire to succeed. Forged by adversity, you stand alongside America's finest special operations forces to serve your country, the American people, and protect their way of life.' You are those men.

"I can't say how proud of all of you I am. You know the greatest thing about being an American is that the United States steps up to the plate sooner than anyone else. And they step up to the plate when others don't.

"The greatest thing about being in the teams is that more is expected of you. And it should be. Every day you live up to that standard. I'm not surprised by that.

"I can tell you the greatest thing about being in my job, at the head of Navy Special Warfare, is that every day I get to go to work with heroes. That's something I believe, something I know. I've seen it.

"You should all look around you. You are surrounded by heroes. That common man with uncommon desire to succeed, that handful of courageous men, you are them.

"We will always remember our team mates who gave their all. But also recognize the strong will, the character and the courage of the man that stands next to you while he's there.

"You will never fail. Thank you."

August 9, 1998-

For there is nothing covered, that shall not be revealed;
Neither hid, that shall not be known.
--Luke 12:2

My Adam got his way! I dated Connar for nine months, then we were married. We all loved the fish farm and him.

Connar asked that I have just one more child, as he had none. Last year I gave birth to Austen Edward.

Although I had my tubes tied for the second time after Austen's birth, somehow I am due to have baby number nine, January 21st of next year. God DOES have a sense of humor!

This one will be a girl. We will call her Angel Rae.

As amazing as this news of our miracle baby was, I was even more shocked by a different discovery. It has been revealed to me that the Mormon Church doctrine is not true!

How could this be? All those life altering decisions that I had made for myself and my children were based on lies!

If I did not understand God's mercy and forgiveness, I would plunge forever into a sea of guilt!

October 6, 2010-

And I will pray the Father,
And he shall give you another Comforter,
That He may abide with you forever;
--John14:15

Captain Symenski, the man who had spoken at Adam's funeral, was the next to give a message. He said he represented the three fallen from the east coast, Group II.

He reminded us that three days from now would be the tenth anniversary of the attack on the USS Cole and that, three days past, was the seventeenth anniversary of the Battle of Mogadishu.

I was disheartened to think that someday I would be remembering this dark moment.

"Today is the tenth or seventeenth anniversary of Adam's accident," I will cry. Could it be possible that I could survive that long on this earth without one of my children? I know it was not with compassion for all the other lives that were lost that I pondered those tragic events, but for my own loss.

"I ask you to keep our fallen heroes in your thoughts and prayers throughout today's service."

I hung my head with shame.

Captain Symenski went on to thank many people. He was grateful for the Heritage Building where we had met that morning and would return after the memorial. He said it had been christened the night after this tragic accident.

We learned that the Heritage Building was not a military building, but was the product of a forty year dream of the community and private donors.

"We gather together once more to memorialize our fallen comrades. And show their families how much we and a grateful Nation honor their service and sacrifice.

"I have a message to the entire Naval special warfare community and to the families of our fallen warriors that I'd like to deliver. But I first want to publicaly provide a few thank you's to a number of people, units, and organizations. And recap the services of the last week to provide some perspective on that message.

"The Patriot Guard was amazing. They stood vigil 24/7, provided escort and emotional and physical protection beyond the call of duty.

"Many of its members are from an era in our country when most were not afforded the same sort of honor and welcome home that our fallen have received from this citizenry. (Pastor Scott had pointed that fact out back in Missouri.)

"The Patriot Guard arrived at every memorial service in force. They stood through watch and escorted our brave and fallen team mates with dignity and humility, ensuring that our fallen heroes were received with the utmost respect.

"Patriot Guard, thank you from the bottom of my heart."

January 4, 1999-

> Train up a child in the way he should go:
> And when he is old, he will not depart from it.
> --Proverbs 22:6

Always remember that the grass may look greener on the other side of the fence, but you still have to mow it! My marrying Connar SEEMED like the answer to all my problems. But I'm just in a different, difficult relationship.

He is not too abusive, he is just not here. I should join a hunter's widow club. He hunts all the time. I wish my concerns were as easy as me just being moody and

110

pregnant but it is far worse than that.

My relationship with Adam has become very strained these days too. He tends to lead the other children in every way, including disrespect. I can almost pin point the day he was first openly rude to me. I had picked him and Andy up at one of the pond dams to take them to town. Jokingly, I'd made some pun-remark as I always do.

Adam laughed and said, "That was stupid."

Andy chimed in, "Yah, that was stupid."

My children had never used the word 'stupid' to me before. Instead of reprimanding them both, I burst into tears. Connar came up to the truck and asked what was wrong, but no one told him. Since then, it has become a bad habit for Adam to talk back to me. Will this only last through the teen years?

I am due to have Angel in a couple weeks and I'm miserable! The house is full of my children again. The three little girls had been at my mother's house for the weekend. Adam and Andy spent a few days with the Dalrymples.

School was cancelled today so the children went out to play in the snow. We now have a long snow tunnel out by pond seven. Everyone is worn out. They are in front of the TV playing Nintendo. I made hot chocolate and caramel corn for them.

No one is fighting. TODAY will go down as a success, as far as the children are concerned anyway.

October 6, 2010-

And whatsoever ye do in word or deed,
do all in the name of the Lord Jesus,
giving thanks to God and the Father by Him.
--Colossians 3:17

"Second," Captain Symansky continued, "I want to thank the Gold Star Mothers."

This is an organization I had not heard about until now, and for good reason. The Gold Star Mothers are those women who have lost a child to war. Although proud to carry the name, none ever wanted the position. I now join them.

"Their shared experiences of losses of their own loved ones, and their outpouring of support and love for our fallen warriors' mothers and families, were amazing. I'm sure that each service has brought painful memories of their own experiences. But they cast aside selflessly and tenderly welcome into their fold with love and support, these mothers now experiencing the pain and sadness of losing a son.

"Gold Star Mothers, your compassion is exemplary. Thank you for your support to our community." The Captain went on to thank the funeral home directors and the regional military units.

I reached up and touched the pin I wore on my lapel, a gold angel with a trident on the front of it. It was a gift from the Gold Star Mothers. I would cherish it, knowing exactly what it signified.

Our sons are with the angels now.

May 23, 1999-

> (Love) Beareth all things, believeth all things,
> hopeth all things, endureth all things.
> --1 Corinthians 13:7

Could my family be falling apart? Am I the only one who cares? Or, are the teenagers taking over?

Amber has graduated from high school and now plans on going to a Mormon college in Idaho. This is against my wishes.

"But, my friends are going there!" she says.

Will she actually choose a school just because her friends are going there?

Audrey still has another year of high school. I have literally taken a shot gun after her criminal boyfriend. He is in prison for a time, but claims he will come back for her. Now his mother is stalking her, even at school. She actually went to the school and had Audrey sign a paper to open a joint checking account with her son! Who is this woman? They can't have my baby!

Then, there is Adam, my first born son. I had so many hopes and dreams for him! He is going through some major rebellion. How my heart breaks.

He has gotten into the teen troubles that some boys do. That I can expect. But when is it time to make some changes?

"I hate you!" he told me the other night.

"How can you say that to me?" I asked

"You always try and act so tough!"

"Someone has to act tough. I'm not the one who was suspended from school with only two days left!"

"Throwing food in the lunch room was a dumb reason to suspend somebody."

"It's not a dumb reason when it is not the first time you've done it. With all your other stunts, they said they are just tired of seeing you in the office. What exactly is your problem? What do you want, Buddy?"

"I don't want any rules!"

"Well, you're too young for that, so that's not going to happen. Now, I have been making some phone calls and I think it will help if you spend the summer with the Dalrymples, or with Grandma and Grandpa. Both would like you to come, so which do you want?"

"I'll go to Grandma and Grandpa's. Call them! Call them now!"

I know we both regretted our angry words to each other. Adam went to the Dalrymples for a few days, then came home to pack for Gene and Lucille's. He remained silent until he was leaving.

"Bye, Mom," he told me. Then he forgot something and ran into the house. When he came out he told me goodbye again and hugged me.

It was like an apology to me for all the harsh words he had thrown in the past. I wanted to shout that I didn't want him to go, but felt it would be best for the summer.

As he rode away, I felt like the proverbial apron string was more than loosened. It was actually torn from my body!

October 6, 2010-

> And all the days of Methuselah were
> nine hundred sixty and nine years:
> And he died.
> --Genesis 5:27

Captain Symensky remembered to thank everyone who had helped our four families. I felt as if I were in a fog. If the show of gratitude were left up to me, I would be sure to miss thanking some generous, kind deed.

It was very pleasing to hear his tribute to the CACOs, the Casualty Assistance Calls Officers. If you have a loved one die while on duty, these military personnel are valuable resources and support. I believe our family was especially blessed with Matt as our CACO.

"The title sounds rather cold and unemotional," the Captain informed the crowd. "But, after witnessing what these CACOs have done for these families, the acronym has a new significance. Warmth and compassion are what they bring to their job and to these families.

"I've spoken to every CACO, whether man or woman, and none of them would ever want to perform in this capacity again. It's like going through BUDS or the Naval Academy. You never want to have to do it again.

"But, the experience is life altering, and oddly fulfilling and enriching, despite the nature of the task assigned. All were trained; none were completely prepared for the magnitude of the challenges. But all rose gracefully to the occasion.

"They grieved with the families, shared intimate family recollections, laughed when the family laughed, remained focused on their task, and ultimately, became an extended member of the family.

"They represented our fallen warriors, their families, their commands, and Naval Special Warfare with grace and professionalism."

He named each CACO and the family he represented. I knew each person in our family had already become closely tied to Matt. Very soon we would have to let him go, too.

"Don't start crying," I told myself. "You may not be able to stop."

114

August 15, 1999-

As we said before, so say I now again,
If any man preach any other gospel unto you
than that ye have received,
Let him be accursed.
--Galatians 1:9

I was baptized today. This makes the third time.

First, as a child, I gave my life to the Lord and was baptized in Shelbyville, Missouri.

That baptism did not count, I was later told by the Mormons. It was not granting me membership into the Mormon Church and was not performed by a priesthood holder. So I allowed them to baptize me again.

Now, today, at the Hurdland City Lake, I was immersed in the water once again. This action did not grant me forgiveness of sins or eternity in heaven. What it did do was to show myself, and others, and my God, that I am truly sorry for following after false gods and that I am truly forgiven! I had gone forward in church months ago to repent and welcome the Lord back into my life.

I had waited for this baptism until everyone was home to witness it. Finally, the family was back together.

Adam was not the only one to spend the summer with his grandparents. Andy felt he couldn't be without Adam. I sent him there too, and they did well. During one of our phone calls, Adam told me he loved me. His grandmother even said he went forward at church camp!

Could our problem have been that Satan suspected we were headed towards God, and wanted to stop us? I don't think he bothers those who don't care.

If I'm right, then there could be even darker days ahead of us!

October 6, 2010-

This know also,
That is the last days perilous times shall come.
--2 Timothy 3:1

115

"If you're getting itchy about the length of my remarks," Captain Symensky continued, "or, where I am going with this, I ask for your patience and understanding for just a few more minutes.

"It is important that we do this right. There is nothing more important right now than taking the time to pay a final tribute to our fallen teammates. I apologize in advance to the families if there are some inaccuracies in my recollection of events of the past week.

"But, in the words of my sister-in-law, 'never let the truth get in the way of a good story.' He began to tell of each of the funerals he and the Master Chief had attended, beginning with Denis Miranda.

"We learned of a proud and close knit family whose father and mother emigrated to the U.S. from Argentina over two decades ago. And whose father worked two jobs to provide for his wife and three boys.

"We learned of and heard stories from Denis' friends, classmates, and fellow lifeguards, on the life changing influence Denis had on them.

"We learned of a mother's love and Patricia's cooking which provided sustenance, and a few pounds, to a number of witnesses.

"Finally, we learned of a brother's love for brother, from Kevin and Allen. We heard stories of contests, challenges, fights, also sibling rivalry and support.

"We witnessed a Veteran of Foreign Wars service at the wake. It was unforgettable. There were men from Tom Brokaw's greatest generation. Men in their twilight years, who had lived, fought, and served in some of the world's bloodiest conflicts in the last century, who came to honor, and pay respect, and recognize another great generation; Denis'. At the funeral that was held the next day, the turnout of people was incredible."

The second funeral that was held was that of Senior Chief David Blake McLendan. He had been a combat support technician to the SEAL team. Due to a storm, the Captain and his colleagues had raced to the service with just minutes to spare.

"At this service, we listened to beautiful hymns and music from Blake and Kate's friends from Virginia Beach. We heard a wonderful message of support from

116

Representative Bishop.

"We listened to meaningful and appropriate scripture from Timothy on 'running the race, fighting the good fight, and keeping the faith,' and from Romans on 'suffering and affliction which bears perseverance, perseverance which bears proven character, and proven character which bears hope. And that does not disappoint'.

"We listened to a friend give testimony to Blake's childhood adventures and his passage into manhood, followed by a brave and bold eulogy by Kate, describing their relationship and what Blake meant to her."

The Captain described the route to the cemetery, lined with citizens standing shoulder to shoulder, holding flags and signs, with hands to hearts in honor of Blake's sacrifice.

"Next we traveled to Macon, Missouri to attend Special Warfare Operator 2nd Class, Adam Olin Smith's funeral and internment service."

My heart began to pound! What did Captain Symansky remember about my son's funeral?

"It was a sunny, blustery day in Macon. We attended the funeral service where we once again heard hymns. One solo was about traveling a different path. It was very powerful and fitting for Adam.

"We heard testimony from the assistant pastor on Adam's childhood. We heard about his childhood pranks, and his family's calls to the Macon County Sheriff's office to apologize for some of that mischief.

"We listened to beautiful passages from a mother's journal, hoping for and forecasting a special calling that she foresaw for Adam.

"We heard a heartfelt sermon from the Pastor on Adam finding his faith. He also quoted scripture in a way I had never heard before at a funeral service, and, in a way that SEALs and Special Operators can truly appreciate."

I was so humbled that the Captain recounted Pastor Scott's Bible stories. It was my hope for Adam's final public tribute to reach the hearts and minds of as many as possible for the Lord! Who in the room would not be touched by the Spirit?

"He spoke of the adventures of King David's 'special operators,' recalling one of their daring exploits through enemy lines to gather a cup of water from the gates of Bethlehem, which he, in turn, poured on the ground in honor of their heroic actions.

"We heard a moving eulogy from one of Adam's SEAL Team Four platoon mates.

"Next we moved to the cemetery, once again escorted by local police and the Patriot Guard. And, once again, the community showed up in full support, lining the local streets, sporadically dispersed along the highway and standing tall for the last half mile into the cemetery."

Although I was proud of each of the SEALs who had sacrificed their lives, I still wanted the Captain to continue talking about Adam. There was so much more to him and about him the crowd didn't know. I'm sure the other mothers felt the same way about their sons.

The last funeral account was that of Lieutenant Brendan Looney. His family had chosen to lay him to rest at Arlington National Cemetery. What an honor. The CACO estimated around four thousand people had visited the wake, including the Governor. Mr. Looney was an excellent lacrosse player.

The priest quoted from Job during the service. Captain Symansky thought it fitting that, at the graveside, when the flags were handed to his wife and mother, the sun chose at that moment to peer from the clouds in a "ray of hope."

October 8, 1999-

When I was a child, I spake as a child,
I understood as a child, I thought as a child:
But when I became a man, I put away childish things.
--1 Corinthians 13:11

Adam turns sixteen today! I want it to be a memorable day for him. He will be home at noon from his friend, Matt's house. I'm going to take him to Kirksville to order a letter jacket. I can't really afford it, but he is counting on it. Later tonight I am picking up Obie and Clark to spend the weekend.

After I clean house today and homeschool, I promised a homeschooler friend I would bring the little ones by for a visit. Then I will get them cleaned up for the trip to Kirksville and to pick up the boys. I feel tired just thinking about it.

Do my children have any idea how much I love them?

October 6, 2010-

> For Thou art my lamp, O Lord:
> And the Lord will lighten my darkness.
> --2 Samuel 22:29

"So, what is my message?" asked Captain Symansky. "It took four funerals over the course of six days for it to become clear to me. As we looked the communities in the eye during these moving and inspirational moments of outreach, as we interacted with them, the full extent of their appreciation for our service, your service, became crystal clear.

"Without exception, they requested that we keep doing what we are doing. These communities believe, like many of us, that service to country is performed for greater causes, greater than self. And members of their very own communities stand for that cause.

"They recognize the sacrifices you make every day. And that you are prepared to lay down your life for your country, your teammate, and the ideals and principles of this great country, particularly freedom.

"America stands behind you and supports you. America believes in you. America has hope and faith in you.

"How do we continue to sustain the trust and hope of our citizens? We do it by continuing to serve and continuing to keep doing what we are doing.

"How do we meet the communities' expectations for our service and uphold our reputation? We uphold our legacy through humble and loyal service to country, team and teammate.

"How do we honor the memory of Brendan, Blake, Adam and Denis? We honor them by continuing our mission with discipline, determination and conviction.

"The country asks this of you. I ask this of you. Stay in the fight. Keep the faith.

To the Looney family, the McLendan family, the Smith and Jorgenson families, and the Miranda family, the community offers our deepest condolences and its vow of support and remembrance.

"Your families now share a common bond, forged by suffering, sacrifice and a loss of your precious gifts.

"Naval Special Warfare people are our greatest asset. You and your families are a part of our people. We have tremendous resources and support from the community. Please reach out to us and ask for our support. We'll do whatever it takes.

"You will remain in our thoughts and prayers and your loved ones will take their rightful, eternal place amongst our fallen heroes, perpetuate our legacy and heritage of service above self.

"God bless you.

"God bless America."

March 11, 2000-

> For by grace are ye saved through faith;
> And that not of yourselves:
> It is the gift of God.
> --Ephesians 2:8

Now Adam is gone.

His anger was getting out of control again. In trouble for the third time with the law, he didn't seem to care! I tried to get through to him, but his anger ran too deep. When he fought multiple times at school, they had no choice but to suspend him. This, in turn, cost him his position on the basketball team, which was my last hope of an influence for the good.

At home he was making our lives miserable, too. The three little girls could not even walk past Adam without him smacking them. It got to the point that they would duck every time they came close to him. It was heart breaking.

"Adam, don't hit your little sisters!" I would yell.

"It doesn't hurt them."

"Yes it does! You never had to live in fear of anyone, and they shouldn't either."

120

It appeared as if I were the real target. As soon as I would comment on his negative behavior, the battle was engaged.

Whatever became of my sweet precious son who couldn't fall asleep without hearing his mamma sing to him? And who was this alien yelling at me that looks like him?

Finally, I called Grandma and Grandpa again. They agreed to help with him. He could live in Louisiana with them and transfer to Acadiana High. Grandpa would straighten him out.

Connar had no say about it. He wasn't home long enough at a time to notice the spiraling problem. He tried to act like Adam's friend more than a father figure. That was OK to a point, but there had to be some rules and discipline with a teen age boy.

"God forgive me for being a failure with my children!

"Why did You entrust me with so many? And forgive me for even thinking that our home is a much more peaceful place with my Adam away.

"Please work on his heart and keep him safe!"

October 6, 2010-

Woe is me for my hurt!
My wound is grievous: but I said,
Truly this is a grief, and I must bear it.
--Jeremiah 10:19

My mind pondered the message of the Captain as several more officers went to the stage and spoke.

"God bless America." His words rang in my ears.

"Why are we in Afghanistan anyway?" I wondered. "It all seems so unnecessary."

Then I reprimanded myself. "I don't remember anyone asking YOU for permission to carry out ANY covert missions! Adam believed in his team and what they stood for. Besides, what if you were a woman from Afghanistan? You would be grateful for the American support! Now, pay attention to what is going on here. You will be speaking soon."

An officer from the east coast had spoken in respect of Lieutenant Looney. He remembered that, along with our fallen, were five from the Army, a civilian interpreter, and an Afghan soldier. All were from different backgrounds, cultures and careers, yet all stood together.

Someone read a letter from Fleming T. Sullivan, Lieutenant Colonel, US Army. It was his hope that this memorial would begin to bring healing to us all. He reminded us that freedom is worth living and dying for, and of our importance to the people of Afghanistan.

"See," I told myself.

In no time at all, the bestowing of the SEALs' awards and medals was upon us. Could my Adam really have completed fifteen missions? I was so surprised that I hardly noticed the tokens of valor as they were shown to me.

"Oh, no, it's time!" I felt panic rise up inside me as it was announced we would hear from team mates and families of the fallen.

"Father, I'm so afraid! Who am I to speak in front of all these people! Please give me strength!"

A team mate of Brendan Looney told stories of Brendan as his swim buddy and best friend on teams. I liked how he described him: "his actions always spoke louder than words", and "the NSW, as a whole, got considerably weaker when that helicopter went down."

We listened as Brendan's sister asked him to "please stand watch over us."

Finally, a heartbroken father expressed his condolences to our families and almost wept as he described Brendan as having taken the path less travelled.

"We are grateful for the time we had with Brendan."

As they sat down and the McLendan family and friends were introduced, I felt faint. We listened to a condensed version of Blake's life. It seems he "got in to just about everything."

We laughed at a story of him tripping over a string of lights, when he was supposed to be quiet and unnoticed.

"I admired his membership in the cryptologic community and his determination to learn Morse code. He too was "inspired to do great things."

Blake's father-in-law touched my heart when he read John 15:13 from the Bible.

"Greater love hath no man than this, that a man lay down his life for his friends."

September 21, 2001-

> Thou hast called me as in a solemn day
> my terrors round about,
> So that in the day of the Lord's anger
> none escaped nor remained:
> Those that I have swaddled and brought up
> hath mine enemy consumed.
> --Lamentations 2:22

On the 11th of this month our country's New York City was attacked by terrorists! Four planes were hijacked. Two were crashed into the twin towers of the World Trade Center. One then crashed into our Pentagon! A forth crashed before it reached the White House! Thousands of people were killed! We will be going to war as soon as we find out who caused all this. God, help those families who were destroyed! And, as our President Bush said, "God bless America!"

I wish my children were all around me now!

Amber quit at the Mormon college and is now renting an apartment in Kirksville! It's a tiny, cute place above a laundromat and next to a fire station, somewhat of a safe spot. She got really burned out from school and never completed her associate degree. Each time she applied for graduation, she was told she needed to take more classes.

Audrey's boyfriend has been in jail again, this time for fighting at a bar. His victim claims he was robbed, too. If convicted, Dill Weed could get up to ten years in prison! Poor Audi, guess he never thought about her.

Adam, I miss greatly! He will be eighteen in two weeks! That is the age he could get drafted! I don't want my boys to go to war! I once felt as if they would be little forever. Playing 'Army' was cute then. It is too real now.

Adam did come home for several days in August. He was a different boy! I took him and Andy to a movie and we actually got along well. I love those boys so much!

Andy is working on getting his license! He is a good driver, though maybe a bit too cautious. I don't seem to worry about him as much as I do Adam. Andy is cautious about many things, and that will serve him well.

Jeffrey has married again, this time to a witch. They have been trying to take my Abbie, Allie and Anna away for a year now through the courts. It is getting old. They don't know who they are dealing with here!

Austen Edward is four! He loves trains and water towers! What a joy.

Angel Rae is just over eighteen months. I rarely find her without a pen in her hand! She holds it perfectly too! I just wish I could locate her stash. She is too young to be going around carrying ink pens.

What about this third marriage of mine? Well, it is hard to explain. We don't really fight, because we never see each other. I may see him sleeping on the couch or driving by in the car or pickup. Or, if I get energetic, I could surprise him and go down to the duck blind where he and his friends are always 'working.' They never seem to make any progress on it. I did that once, and found out way more than I wanted to know. It seems that he smokes more than regular cigarettes.

How have I dealt with that? I am ignoring it.

What else can I do? I have too many children to start over again. Where can I go?

Would he even notice that we were gone?

October 6, 2010-

And thou shalt love the Lord thy God with all thine heart,
And with all thy soul, and with all thy might.
--Deuteronomy 6:5

My legs felt like rubber as my name was announced to speak for my Adam. Little Wally also made his way to the stage. As we ascended the stairs, I whispered to him to speak first. I knew he would, but again I felt panic rise inside of me.

"I was just one of Adam's many friends," he began. He informed everyone that he had only met Adam a few years

124

ago, when they were both assigned to a climbing school in Colorado.

"We weren't there long before I realized, 'Hey, this Adam Smith guy is pretty cool.' Sooner or later we started to hang out together, working out, drinking beer together. Most of the time we probably drank a few more beers than we should have. Adam was a bad influence on me." (The audience laughed.)

"One of the last things we did at the course was, we climbed Mt. Quandary. Quandary was a 14,000 feet plus mountain. When we got to roughly 13,000 feet, Adam happened to have vehicle keys. The instructors wanted everyone with vehicle keys to go back down the mountain. So, meanwhile, the rest of us reached the summit.

"Immediately, when I got back down, I made two groups. There was the Team Summit, and there was the Non Summiters: Adam. I was relentless with him. Every time we did anything it was 'Hey, Team Summit. Team Summits going to go get some beers, etc...' Of course Adam was excluded.

"Eventually, Adam got so bothered by not being in Team Summit that the day we were leaving, he called up his airline. He's like, 'Hey, I need a flight out the next day.'

"He tells us, 'Hey guys, I'm gonna climb that stupid mountain.' The next day, of course, he goes up there and climbs it by himself! He's up on the top taking 'happy snaps' of himself. You know, just for evidence, so he can prove he was up there.

"That's exactly how Adam was. He gave everything he had and left nothing on the field.

"Adam loved being a 'team guy' and he was damn good at it. He was the backbone of his platoon. It didn't surprise me when I found out that the majority of new guys in his platoon, when they were questioned in the review board, 'Who would they most want to be like?' they responded, 'Adam'.

"Jack said it best, though, at Adam's funeral service. Adam was 99% of the time, humble. That 1% of the time is when we were playing X Box. Adam was ridiculous playing X Box. He was just running his mouth the whole time!" (Wally made motions with his hand of a duck quacking.)

"There were a few times where I almost threw the controller at his head from about five feet away from him! I knew his tricks though. He wasn't that good at HALO. He was just a habitual screen watcher."

The crowd roared with laughter. I'm not a gamer so I didn't understand the meaning of Wally's words. But I was pleased for everyone to have a small glimpse of my son's easy going life, when he did have a moment to relax.

"Everyone who knew Adam," continued Wally, "knew that, if there was a dull moment, he would lay back and just smile in his nonchalant attitude about everything.

"But they also knew Adam was quick to throw mitts. Adam had a vicious right hook. And, unfortunately for those on the receiving end, they'd usually be sleeping after the first hit. 'Cause Adam would be quick to follow with a second and a third."

Wally stopped for a moment and took a deep breath.

"Adam had my back while he was here. And, I know he will continue to do so, along with all our brothers in arms over seas.

"Mr. Smith, Mrs. Jorgenson, it was truly an honor and a privilege to have known your son and been his friend. Thank you.

"Adam, I'll never forget you, Buddy."

December 4, 2001

> For God hath not given us the spirit of fear;
> But of power, and of love, and of a sound mind.
> --2 Timothy 1:7

When will I learn that I should not think of my life as being so very awful? It can always get worse!

I am now sleeping on my mother's floor at her house in Bevier. I have the five younger children here with me. Andy is staying at the Dalrymple's until I can find a place for us. How did this happen?

On November 16th our world turned upside down. I was so worried about terrorists that I forgot what was going on in my own home. I stumbled right into the middle of it. I could ignore it no longer!

For weeks Connar had been avoiding us like the plague. When he was home he either slept or looked for tiny little reasons to blow up at us.

I could not do anything right. I continued to tell myself he was just worn out.

When I went to tell him it was lunch time that day, he acted so nervous to have me around the old hog confinement building. I went back later, thinking I would find he had been smoking cigarettes again. What I found were bags, scales and piles of brown plants. I panicked.

Instead of telling Connar what I knew, I asked him if he would do anything to jeopardize my custody battle for the girls. He looked at me with his blood shot eyes and said, "No." I knew then I needed to talk to someone else.

The year before, when I had discovered him smoking pot, I had confided in our family friend, the sheriff, about it. He said just continue to watch him. I thought that was odd, but agreed since it meant not disrupting my family.

This time I actually showed him some of the plants. He wasn't so forgiving. He told Connar he had to arrest him since I had shown it to him. Somewhere within a few short days, I became the bad guy to everyone! I even had Christian people tell me I was wrong to do that.

On top of that, Jeffrey and his wife found out I was staying in Bevier. They called DFS and told them they saw my children running in the street barefoot and without coats. I was called in to report my abilities as a mother!

"When are you going to find a house of your own?" my mother just asked me again!

It's been three weeks!

God help me! I've done nothing wrong!

October 6, 2010-

Watch therefore:
For ye know not what hour your Lord doth come.
--Matthew 24:42

Little Wally finished and turned to me. We botched a hug, which lightened our moods a bit. Then I stepped up to the podium. For the first time I looked out into the audience. I almost gasped. Hundreds of faces stared back at me!

"I can't believe I volunteered for this," I began. "I'm just a mom."

I thanked all those who made it possible for my family to be there and for the kindness shown to us.

"Getting to know Adam's SEAL family and friends, and Charlotte, has actually begun our healing process. You see, we have a million memories of Adam growing up.

"He was so ornery. And, he only learned to swim in ponds and lakes. We don't have oceans back in Missouri.

"But, he didn't get home much as an adult, so our picture of him was kind of incomplete. Getting to know everyone has helped us get to know the man he became, and we are really pleased.

"Different stories have popped up recently. On our way up here, a woman called and said she had served with Adam in Iraq. She said he always did everything with a smile on his face, no matter what.

"Just yesterday I met someone in transportation. You know, I just want to cling to anything anyone has to say about Adam. So I asked this man in transportation, 'Did you know my son?'

"He said he'd only met him a few times, but he was always impressed that he wasn't too proud to help clean the vehicles. I guess that's something not everybody does. (There was great laughter in the audience. I guessed that I had hit on a spot of light conflict.)

"So, you have completed our picture, and we are grateful for that.

"We want you to know, especially the SEALs, that every night our family kneels in prayer. No matter where you are at in the world, there's going to be a family in Macon, Missouri that's going to be praying for you-- for your salvation and your safety.

"I've read my Bible since I was a little girl. I still can't memorize verses, but I know what's in there. The moment I heard what happened to my son, this verse came into my mind: '...all things work together for the good for those that love Him...' (Romans 8:28).

"I thought, Lord, I love You, but how in the world could You work something like this to the good? How could You do that?

"You know what? In the past couple weeks I've started to see some good, believe it or not, come out of this.

"I just thank you all for the part you've had in my son's life. We're going to miss him so much! He was our hero!

"Thank you and God bless you."

January 12, 2002-

O Lord, thou knowest:
Remember me, and visit me,
and revenge me of my persecutors;
Take me not away in thy longsuffering:
Know that for thy sake I have suffered rebuke.
--Jeremiah 15:15

Well, things have gotten "better?" I have rented a house behind the Bait House in Bevier. I am working there for my landlord a few nights a week as well as on the ambulance for Macon County.

For now at least, all nine of my children are home! Amber is threatening to move to Provo, Utah. She is in "like" with a Mormon named Adam, and he wants her out there until he can decide if he wants to marry her or not. Sounds like a plan!

Audrey has left her "worse half" again and is now looking for a job here.

Adam is finally home! His friends all asked if we could talk him into finishing his senior year here at Bevier. He actually asked me if he could do it, when I called him. I just wish I had another vehicle he and I could share.

Andy is beginning to run around some. I am uncomfortable when I don't know where my children are.

Abbie and Allie are both playing basketball! They had their first practice today. The coach said they did well.

Anna is doing well in school. I had feared for my children, returning to public school after homeschooling them. But I should not have worried. A certified teacher tested them for me, only to find that they are right at the level I placed them. The school did not believe me, though, and took them from class for a week to test them. Low and behold, they placed them again where I said they were. Praise the Lord!

And, what about little Austen and Angel? They are suffering because of their foolish parents, as well as the other children. Still, they remain sweet and innocent.

Our lives have become such a drama. There is noise and discord and anger. Most of it is directed at me. Everyone, (except me), thinks they would be happier if I took Connar back. My own counselor told me that it would be worse than before. It would not be safe.

I've got to hold it all together. I would consider some sort of medication to help me through this, but I have always made it before without drugs.

God is my Prozac!

October 6, 2010-

> Heaven and earth shall pass away,
> But my words shall not pass away.
> --Matthew 24:35

There was a tremendous amount of applause as Wally and I returned to our seats. I think everyone was just surprised a mother could still function within such a short time of tragedy. I can only claim that the power was from God. I could hear myself speaking, and feel myself moving, yet it was as if my heart was cracked and about to burst.

I closed my mind's door to my grief, as I would learn to do quite well, and became attentive to what was going on around me.

Our Jack went up then to speak in behalf of Denis Miranda. He carried a message from his troop commander from Afghanistan.

"He wanted me to pass the message to you all. From SEAL Team 4, two troop, the Horsemen, to the families: our prayers and thoughts are always with you. Our troop wishes they could be here. And, we'll never forget.

"To SEAL Team 3 brothers, it was our honor and

privilege to serve with you for the short time that we had together.

"Now let me get to business," Jack smiled. "Old Denis Miranda, let me tell you about this guy. He was a special breed of warrior. He was one of those warriors that shaved his arms and his chest."

Everyone laughted.

"I'm pretty sure he shaved his legs too.

"First time I met Denis, he checked in to our platoon, and he didn't fare so well at 18th Delta.

"Getting to know Denis was a privilege. Everything with Denis with work was always, 'yes, sir and no sir.' It didn't matter if you were enlisted or an officer, he showed everybody respect.

"I always called Denis a kid even though I'm only a week and a half older than him. It was that he was a new guy and young.

"Even to the days leading up to this op, I got to spend a lot of time with Denis, Adam and Blake and Looney.

"Denis, being the new guy that he was, was so ambitious. He was such a great guy that we actually gave him a sniper rifle. We gave him a Mark Eleven. And we started teaching him how to use it.

"I'm a pretty early riser. I was getting up around six in the morning. He was up at, like five. He lived right across from me. He would have everything ready to go-- rifle, ammo, targets, everything we needed to go to the range. He was like a little kid on Christmas ready to open up presents.

"He was like, 'when are we going, hey, when are we going?'

"And he'd do the same thing to Adam. 'Hey, Adam, when are we going to the range?'

"It never ended. That's how he was about work. He took everything so serious.

"That night, I walked into his room. I go, 'Denis.'

"Yes, sir!" pants down to the floor."

The room filled with laughter.

"Still didn't pick up his pants.

"I go, 'Uh, what are you doing?'

"On his bed was his kit, uniform and everything. It was just ready to go.

"I said, 'Hey, brother, you need to get some sleep, man.

We're gonna have a long night.

"I went to bed. LT woke me up to look at some stuff. I walked into the 'talk' (conference room) and there Denis is in the 'talk,' full uniform, and working on his kit. He didn't sleep a wink. He was so excited.

"And that's just how Denis was. He was so excited about life and about the Teams."

Jack took us even farther back to when he was at Key West, learning how to be a dive supervisor.

"I had to stand up in front of everybody. I had my hat on backwards, and there I was giving this brief. At the end of this brief, I go, 'Are there any questions?'

"That's when Denis stands up. He says, 'hey, Jack.'

"I say, 'yah, what's up, man.'

"He said. 'How do you get the back of your hair to touch the back of your brim?'

"Sure enough, the next day the Chief…well, I was in the barber shop getting my hair cut. I had to thank Denis for that one later. I gave him a real good 'thank you.'

"That very same trip, I happened to clean up the classroom. There were some notebooks lying around. I grabbed Denis' notebook to, you know, I was going to hide it from him. Just to give him a little 'something.'

"I opened it up thinking that there would be drawings, because Team guys don't like diving. We just, you know, don't pay attention and we draw. There could be all sorts of stuff in there.

"You know what? It was a testament to Denis that, while I was giving a brief, he was writing down everything I was saying. It wasn't just the important stuff like when we take CQC, land warfare, sniping, breeching, or all those things that we hold dear to our hearts as Team guys that makes us who we are. There Denis is, taking notes about diving. And that's just the kind of guy Denis was.

"Nathaniel Hawthorn wrote this, 'All brave men love. For he only is brave who has affections to fight for, whether in the daily battle of life or in physical contest.'

"Denis was all those things. He was a brave man. And, he was quick to throw punches. I don't know if that's because he was in Adam's squad or if that's just because he was from Jersey."

Jack told the audience about going to meet Denis'

family, and how much they impressed him with their concerns for his needs in their time of tragedy.

"Denis was a great brother. He was a great son. He was a great fiancé and he was a great teammate. I'm never going to forget Denis.

"So to Adam and Denis, and to Blake and Looney- the Horsemen, we will all ride together. We love you."

July 6, 2002-

Rejoice not against me, O mine enemy:
When I fall, I shall arise;
When I sit in darkness, the Lord shall be a light unto me.
--Micah 7:8

Where has the time gone? I look at my three fine sons and am so humbled. Two are almost grown!

My Adam has already graduated from high school! It was a good ceremony. Somehow he and Obie managed to convince those in authority to let them walk side by side. I was so proud of him!

When it came time for the graduates to exit, they met each other in the front of the room and walked out by twos. When Adam and Obie met back up, they pounded fists in a gesture as if to say, "We did it!" It was awesome!

Adam is spending some time this summer with his dad. He is angry at me for divorcing Connar. I will probably never tell him that it was Connar who had the separation agreement changed into a divorce. Adam is just hurt.

Andy is actually coming home every night by ten o'clock. It really helps that he is going out with the daughter of one of my friends. When I think of it, Andy hasn't really given me many problems. Yes, the usual boy stuff, but nothing compared to his older brother.

Then there is my little Austen. He turned five years old today. He reminds me so much of Adam. He asked me last night if I would measure how tall he was the moment he woke up. How cute.

This morning I went for an early workout at the YMCA while the little ones were still asleep. When I returned home I found everyone was awake. It seems Austen awoke after I left and asked, "Where's Mom?"

The girls told him where I was and he said, "You can't start a birthday without Mom!"

I love that guy!

October 6, 2010-

> I wait for the Lord, my soul doth wait,
> And in His word do I hope.
> --Psalm 130:5

Jack turned and hugged Denis' brother who then approached the podium. He sent out his and his family's condolences. He began to cry.

"Denis achieved his goals, did his dream job. Not only did he want to fight for his country, but he wanted to serve his country and be part of the reason we can all sleep at night with freedom flowing through our minds.

"Denis accomplished something that not many have. He was a United States Navy SEAL at work, but at home he was a son, the oldest of three brothers, a best friend and fiancé to a beautiful woman.

"Today I speak to you on behalf of my oldest brother. Denis was born a leader..."

My mind began to notice a pattern with these brave Navy SEALs. As Denis' brother described him to be a role model, mentor, generous, not materialistic, and more, I realized they were all from the same mold. They were the "chosen."

My attention returned to the service to hear a story of Denis' brother catching him vacuuming one day, completely in the nude!

"I thought, 'Does this really have to be my brother.'"

He finished the story, and everyone laughed. Then he became serious again.

"The idea is not to forget him, but to remember him with every decision I make, with every obstacle I encounter, and with every goal I achieve. My brother was a stud. I love you, man."

January 5, 2003-

That if thou shalt confess with thy mouth the Lord Jesus,
And shalt believe in thine heart
that God hath raised Him from the dead,
Thou shalt be saved.
--Romans 10:9

My first born son was saved tonight! God is truly in control!

I was having an incredibly awful day, thinking only of myself. I had gone to pick up Austen and Angel at their father's house, and he, as usual, was giving me a hard time about everything. Little Austen put on his coat, packed his toys and said, "I'm ready to go."

That put us both in our places.

On the drive home, I cried all the way. I tried to hide it from the two little ones.

When I arrived back at Bevier, I called my mother who was watching the three little girls for me. My sister Amy couldn't wait to tell me what had happened to Adam during youth meeting.

I quickly called him. "Son, I've just heard the most incredible news!"

He was crying. He could hardly speak.

"Buddy, I love you so much!"

He said, "I love you, too!"

He hasn't said that to me in a long, long time!

"God, forgive me for not being the prayer warrior that I could be! Please save ALL my babies!"

October 6, 2010-

For ye were sometimes darkness,
But now are ye light in the Lord: walk as children of light:
(For the fruit of the Spirit is in all goodness
and righteousness and truth;)
Proving what is acceptable unto the Lord.
--Ephesians 5:8-10

The music from the video faded to an end, and the pictures stopped appearing. A Navy chaplain rose to give the benediction and asked us to stand with him.

"As we bring this memorial ceremony to a close, we all have different emotions that flood our hearts at this time, that leave an emotional stamp upon us. Some may be numbed, shocked, angered, and even distressed. But people of faith and of justice have a Comfort throughout the ages."

He restated the Psalm read at the beginning of the ceremony, "God is our refuge and strength, an ever present help in trouble.

"Therefore we will not fear, though the earth give way, and though the mountains fall into the heart of the sea; though its waters roar and foam, and though the mountains quake with their surging. There is a river, whose streams make glad the city of God, the holy place where the Most High dwells.

"God is within her; she will not fall: God will help her at the break of day.

"Nations are in an uproar, kingdoms fall: He who lifts His voice, the earth melts.

"The Lord Almighty is with us; the God of Jacob is our fortress.

"So we close today. May we honor these fallen heroes with our tears, our memories, our uncompromising integrity, a steadfast character, perseverance in adversity, and a renewed vigilance to be warriors who are ready to answer our nation's call, guardians of our fellow Americans and defenders of those who are unable to defend themselves. Let us pray.

"God, our refuge and strength, our ever-present help in trouble, we come to You with heavy, broken hearts as we honor our heroes, Brendan, Blake, Adam and Denis.

"We ask for Your comforting and consoling presence to be near their families and loved ones. Imprint their heritage of love, loyalty and devotion on our hearts so we may live with courage and determination in a confused and broken world.

"May their light be a light that gives us guidance as we are on a quest to bring hope to the darkness that haunts the multitudes.

"And now may the Lord bless you and keep you. May

136

the Lord make His face to shine on you and be gracious to you. The Lord will turn His face toward you and give you His peace, Amen."

July 11, 2003-

Where thou diest, will I die, and there will I be buried:
The Lord do so to me: and more also,
If ought but death part thee and me.
--Ruth 1:17

My poor Adam has felt the heartache of death for the first time in his young life. His dear friend Billy, who had attended Junior High School with him, was tragically killed in an accident today.

I was working the ambulance for Macon County when I got the call from someone in Knox County about Billy. After securing a replacement at work, I located Adam playing basketball with Obie, Clark, and some other friends at the YMCA in Macon. I entered the 'Y' and walked out onto the upper floor track. I could look down onto the gym where they were playing.

For a brief moment, I hesitated to tell Adam. I could see what a great time the old friends were having and knew that in a few short seconds his young life would change forever. Obie spotted me and stopped the game.

"Adam," I called out, "can you come here please?"

He must have heard the pain in my voice, because he immediately ran to the stairs to come to me.

"What's wrong?" Obie tried to find out from the level below me.

All I could say was, "It's about Adam's friend, Billy."

"Mom, what is it?" Adam asked me once he reached the top of the stairs.

"Buddy, I'm so sorry to tell you this, but I got a call a while ago that Billy has been killed."

"What!" he cried, "What happened?"

"I'm not sure but I'm going to his house right now, so I came to get you."

Adam and I left to make the forty minute trip to Billy's house. All the way there, Adam continuously asked me why and how this could have happened. I could only tell him I did not know for sure.

I remembered when they had become friends. Billy was Adam's first friend after we had moved to Knox County. He had been to our house many times, and had Adam over to his house just as many. The boys had attended camps together, and were in the same grade. I will always remember Billy and his two brothers. Whenever I would pull up at their house they would all come out to my car to greet me with those adorable smiles.

It just so happened that Billy's younger brother, Cole, was Andy's best friend and my Andy was actually with Billy's family when the accident happened. Along with answering Adam's questions of grief I was very worried about Andy.

Once we arrived, I was able to find Andy and see that he was unhurt. Then I consoled Billy's family the best I could.

On the ride home the boys were silent. I felt sheer pain for the both of them. Death had never come so close to our family. Where were all my words of wisdom? I was at a loss. I could only pray.

Both the boys are sleeping now. They did not eat anything for supper.

"God, please comfort my sons in their grief!"

October 6, 2010-

Though He slay me, yet will I trust in Him:
But I will maintain mine own ways before Him.
--Job 13:15

My family was escorted back to the vans and driven back to the Heritage Building. Once again I could not relax. I felt tense and angry at everyone. My attitude was such a contrast to those around me. I felt ashamed. The children were even laughing and joking around. I wiped back the tears that threatened to flow.

An awesome lunch was presented to us and I was glad that my hungry family was fed. Even though I fixed a plate for myself, the food seemed to have no taste. I felt as if I would choke.

Many kind people came up to me and complimented me on speaking at the memorial. It helped to calm my nerves.

Several rooms were set up with banquet-sized tables and chairs, with more chairs along the walls. I chose to enter one and sit at a table. I noticed a gentleman in a suit who came into the room and chose to sit apart from all of the families. He sat quietly in one of the chairs away from the table. I felt like he was watching me. I wondered if my family was getting too loud or something.

After a while, when no one was around me for a moment, he came over. He sat down in the next chair and turned towards me!

"I just wanted to tell you that I have attended memorials for many years and played the bagpipes. Of all those ceremonies, I have never been so impressed with what someone has said, as I was with your words today."

I was speechless. Surely he did not mean my poor attempt at oration!

"Well, thank you. I want you to know that I have been so sad to not have gotten to hear the bagpipes at Adam's service. You can imagine how excited and humbled I was when I walked in to hear you playing them today!"

We spoke only a few moments more, and then he disappeared into the crowd. I never saw him again, but will always be grateful to this gentleman.

I realized that I did not recognize anyone in the room. I turned towards the door and in walked Charlotte. She had a sweet looking couple with her.

"Michele, I'd like you to meet my parents."

They were so nice! I remembered that she had told me once that her father read his Bible all the time. I'm not sure why I said it, but then again many words that were coming out of my mouth were strange those days.

"I hear you know your Bible!"

He seemed surprised, and why not?

"Yes, yes I do!" he smiled.

Well, so much for first impressions. But they never gave a clue if they thought I was crazy. That must be where Charlotte learned her mild manners and compassion. I felt sad that we would not have the chance to plan a big wedding some day for our two children.

I'm not sure just what else I said to her parents, but they moved on to speak to others that they knew. I began to feel absolutely exhausted, so I decide to locate my family. They were scattered.

Only two feet outside the doorway I was stopped by a Navy SEAL.

"I was hoping to get to talk to you," he said. "My mother passed away recently."

"I'm so sorry." I told him.

"Well, she used to make the best ice tea. I just know that right now she is in heaven making some tea for Adam."

I was not prepared to hear this. It meant picturing my son in a faraway place, no longer here. I just smiled and nodded my head in agreement.

He then told me how sorry he was for my loss, and his voice cracked a bit when he said, "I have two little boys and I can see what you must be going through when I watch my wife with those boys." He began to cry openly. "She loves those boys so much!"

Of all those around me, he felt some of my pain.

I just hugged him.

December 2, 2003-

He that dwelleth in the secret place of the Most High
Shall abide under the shadow of the Almighty.
--Psalm 91:1

Today I am forty-one years old! What a ride this life has been!

Somehow, and I know it is only by the grace of God, we are making it alone! Who would have thought that my bank would trust me enough to loan me money to buy a house? We love our little place at the edge of Bevier. It has a small orchard and a tiny three bedroom house. The street is peaceful and safe for my children. Praise God!

How do I want to spend this day? Well, it is 5:00 AM and I am up already. I did have a cappuccino late yesterday which may be the reason I can't sleep

It is Tuesday. I will get the five younger children off to school and then take Adam to Kirksville.

Adam has not been doing well since high school. He

finally gave up on the junior college thing. His grades were so low that he could never make it all up. He is only getting into trouble around here. He came to one of Allie's basketball games the other night and his face was all messed up from having been in a fight. My son, why does he feel he needs to settle everything with his fists?

And, now he has begun breaking the law. How many times will a judge see him for silly things, before he has seen him enough?

Already I have gone to court with him over a huge speeding ticket. Adam was in another county with one of his friends. He was driving during the day down a lonely blacktopped road, when he decided to see just how fast his car could go. There was a lone car sitting on a side gravel road a half mile away.

"Wouldn't it suck if that was a cop up there?" he had said to his friend.

Sure enough, it was an officer. I had to go to court with Adam in a county where I knew no one and hoped they would not send my son to jail. That cost Adam his license and a fine, and it cost me more stress too.

Then one night, he and three of his friends decided to go out mail box bashing. This is a deadly "game" some bored teens invented. A passenger in a vehicle will lean way out his window and hit mail boxes with a baseball bat as they pass by them. I don't know if the drivers realize that they hold their passenger's lives in their hands and driving skills. A few inches too close to the box could end all the "fun" for the night.

I believe a total of twenty destroyed mail boxes were reported on the same road in Macon County. The sheriff's department was investigating. Adam's name came up as a possible suspect. I knew they were looking for him to question him.

A few nights later I received call from an officer in a little town twenty minutes from my home.

He identified himself and asked, "Are you the mother of Adam Smith?"

Instantly I burst into tears.

"Is he alright?" I cried.

"Yes, ma'am, Adam is fine. I pulled him over tonight in town and he was very respectful of me and told me he had

141

been drinking right when I asked him. I just need you to come and get him."

"I'll be right there." I said through my sobs.

When I finally arrived at the police station I could hear someone in another room yelling at someone else. I soon realized that it was someone yelling at Adam.

"What kind of man are you to make your mother cry like that! Did you know she started crying right when I called her? She didn't even know what you had done yet. Do you do that to her a lot?" He went on for quite some time.

When I met the officer I was very impressed. He was young and strong and kind. He looked like an example of what every mother would want her son to be like. I was grateful to him. Adam would be facing some charges.

On the way home I had a long talk with Adam. He was truly sorry for the pain he had caused me.

"We have bigger problems right now, Buddy," I told him. "The sheriff wants to talk to you about some mail box stunts."

He confessed to me that he had been with those boys who had hit all the boxes. Adam agreed to let me take him to the sheriff's office and face whatever his punishment would be.

They wanted to keep him in jail over night. I did not sleep the rest of the night. I called several times to see if he were OK. Adam did not sleep either. He said he roomed with an arsonist and a rapist and he did not even go to the bathroom the entire night. By the next morning Adam realized that jail was not the place for him.

I thought, "Finally, has he grown up and learned his lesson?"

The prosecutor felt different. I went up face to face in court with a short wiry female who thought that my son should actually go to prison for destroying other people's mail boxes!

"Tampering with the mail is a federal offense."

When I, in dismay, stated we could not afford an attorney, she just shrugged her shoulders as if to say, "So."

I turned to the judge with pleading eyes. My son had not robbed or murdered or anything like that. And he had turned himself in, too.

142

"Ma'am, we will get you an attorney," the kind judge said. And they did.

Adam was very lucky. At the final judgment, this mail box bashing was not considered a federal offence, since it was done at night and there was no mail in the boxes! The other boys involved were not punished, as they had not turned eighteen yet. Adam did not mention any of their names.

My thoughts on the whole deal were that they should have been made to dig up all the damaged boxes and replace them. When a fine is imposed or a license is taken away, the parents are the ones who suffer more it seems.

I had had enough of Adam's childish pranks and actions. I think he knew it. He stuck to just fighting. That was a cause for enough trouble.

One night I heard Adam being dropped off in my yard. When I investigated I found him with his eye puffed up so big he couldn't open it. He said it was after he had been hit with a bottle in the face.

"Just cut it, Mom," he told me to let some of the pressure off.

"Who do you think you are, Rocky?"

"It wasn't swollen up until I held my nose and blew to clear my sinuses."

I knew that didn't sound right, so I pressed a bit around his face. The feeling of air under his skin made me realize it was more serious than just a black eye.

A trip to the ER and x-rays showed that Adam had fractured his sinuses and was going to need surgery.

"I'm not sure how we are going to pay for this."

"I'll take care of it, Mom."

Even though I did not know how he would pay for it, I felt sure he would.

Adam has been visiting with a Navy recruiter over the phone. I will take him to Kirksville to meet him today. I'm not sure if I trust recruiters. My heart aches at the thought of Adam going into the service, but if every mother held her little boy back, where would our country be?

I am pleased that he will choose the Navy like my dad and uncles.

October 7, 2010-

> Thou therefore endure hardness,
> As a good soldier of Jesus Christ.
> --2 Timothy 2:3

We were driven back to our hotel by the Navy. I decided I would stay in Virginia a few days longer with Amber, Audrey and Andy, to help settle some of Adam's affairs. I was not sure how much help I would be, but I could not leave that soon. I wanted to know about the life my son had been leading on the east coast.

After the memorial, we all went with Charlotte and several of the SEALs to a place called Chicks. It was a pub on the coast where I was told Adam had spent many good times. Adam's picture was set up there, and a book was lying close by for his friends to record memories of him. The mood was festive.

James flew back this morning with four of the younger children, Eric's wife Teresa, and their two children. Eric remained in Virginia. It all seemed kind of awkward, but my husband stood by me in everything I felt like I needed to do to get through this.

The moment James and the children had gone, I felt alone. They had left at a very early hour. I could not stay in bed and think, so I got up, packed, and kept busy until Amber called to say they were ready to leave the hotel and go to Adam's house. Outside we were offered Adam's car to drive to his house. I could not bring myself to ride in it. Matt drove me.

Adam was buying a house with his friend, Josh, who is in Afghanistan. I had pictured it to be right on the beach, but it was a few blocks away in a peaceful little neighborhood.

As we pulled up I could see people outside in their yards, standing around talking. They watched as we entered the house.

We weren't inside very long before several visitors from the area began to drop by to pay their respects to us for Adam. The stories began to flow.

One couple who lived right next door was originally from Scotland. They remembered Adam with love. In their

Scottish accents they recalled my son's kindness to them. They offered to bring over our evening meal.

Another woman came over with a gift of food and told us how Adam had treated her.

"I was out mowing my lawn and doing other yard work one day when I saw Adam come home carrying a bag of groceries. When he saw me, he just set his food down and came right over to help me."

The stories went on and on. I was so proud at the humility and kindness from my son who once seemed so full of anger.

I was given Adam's room upstairs that night. It was the hardest thing ever, to climb those stairs and open that door knowing that I was about to enter a place he had slept in a few weeks before.

I was told that the officials had already been there and removed some things. The rest of his effects were placed in boxes, but the bed was still as he had left it. I felt myself falling apart, and Amber must have noticed it, because she said she was going back down stairs.

I collapsed on Adam's bed and cried. I had been holding it all in for so long.

"Why, why, why?" the familiar words were spoken.

But an answer was not expected.

October 24, 2005-

Love not the world,
Neither the things that are in the world.
If any man love the world,
the love of the Father is not in him.
--1 John 2:15

Oh, how quickly our lives can change! In June some boys from Bevier hurt my baby Allie. They were just under the age of adult, and my lawyer told me it would be worse on her to pursue criminal action against them than to just get her some counseling. My God, has the whole world gone crazy? I could not expect her to attend school in Bevier with these monsters, so I bought a house in Macon and dragged everyone here.

I do not like it here, but that is just me. I'm working for a cardiologist in Moberly and have been able to put Allie into counseling. She will never be the same.

The other children seem to be adjusting to a new school and a new house.

In September, my Andy called to tell me he had joined the Army! He had been staying in his dad's basement since he graduated from High School and wasn't finding work easily in Columbia. Why the Army? That was his choice and I'm proud of him. He called last night to tell me he is doing well and has even gone to church!

Adam graduated from Navy basic training near Chicago. He hurt my feelings deeply then, but I've forgiven him. I spent an entire paycheck to drive all the way there to see him graduate. He had also invited Connar. When the ceremony was over, I saw Adam for maybe fifteen minutes. Connar took him aside and told him he would buy him a steak dinner to celebrate. Then Adam walked back over to me.

"Mom, thank you for coming to my graduation," he said, giving me a hug.

That was it? I cried all the way home, but knew Adam was young and impressionable and that he still loved me.

Money is really tight these days, though. I now have two house payments to make until I can sell the house in Bevier, not to mention a car payment and other bills. I'm not sure what to do when Andy graduates down in Georgia.

Adam is still training for the Navy. He decided to become a Navy SEAL. Now he is in California at BUDS. He has developed pneumonia from breathing in water during the underwater training. If he is not "over it" by today, it will set him back seven weeks!

We pray God's will for him.

October 8, 2010-

> Behold, He cometh with clouds;
> And every eye shall see Him,
> and they also which pierced Him:
> And all kindreds of the earth shall wail
> because of Him. Even so, Amen.
> Revelation 1:7

146

Today is my Adam Olin's 27th birthday. It seems wrong to celebrate but the family and Charlotte and his friends all want to have a party in honor of him. I still want to curl up and die myself, but that is not healthy either. They have chosen to find out where one of Adam's favorite local musicians is singing tonight, and have the party there.

The past few days have gone by so quickly. I have not even helped with calling all of Adam's debtors to inform them of his accident. I thought I could, but when I heard my Amber on the phone yesterday, it broke my heart all over again.

"Hi, I'm calling for my brother, Adam Smith. He has an account with you. I wanted to let you know that he has been killed in Afghanistan....oh, thank you, our family appreciates that...we will be closing that account...I'll give you his account number..."

Each call was another step towards finality in my son's life. I had to go up to his room and cry again. I looked around, and found several Bibles in his room. That pleased me. I made the mistake of reading the Book of Ecclesiastes in his Bible. Never read Ecclesiastes when you are grieving.

Charlotte has been wonderful! She has put aside her own brokenness and tried to show us so much about Adam while we are here. We have learned of their first date. She said Adam had tried so hard to win her a prize at a little carnival and could only win this tiny, pathetic, green, stuffed turtle. She loved it so much she still carried it with her. I took a picture of her sitting at a picnic table at a spot where Adam used to like to take her to eat. She sat there sadly holding onto that little token of their first date.

We have visited a lighthouse, a board walk, and bike riding trails, a basketball court, and many other Adam hang-outs. At every place there would be a moment or two when I could see Charlotte looking at a far off time when Adam actually stood there with her. She suffers as much as we do but in a very recent way.

Father, please help us all learn to live in a world that no longer has our Adam Olin in it.

August 12, 2007-

[Our Lord Jesus Christ]
Who gave Himself for our sins,
That He might deliver us from this present evil world,
According to the will of God and our Father:
--Galatians 1:4

Our lives at home actually got worse before they got better.

I hit bottom financially and spiritually. I quit my job at the cardiologist's office because I was away from home too much every night.

I opened a daycare at my home. That was good for the children but did not pay well. So, on weekends I found sitters for the kids and worked for three different ambulance agencies. There were a few times I did not even have food in the house. Once I took the children to a math night at school, just to get the refreshments for their supper.

I never made it to my Andy's graduation from boot camp! What a horrid mother! He was sent to Washington for a bit, is now in Germany and will soon be in Iraq! I worry more for his safety than for Adam's. Andy's training was so brief and soon he will be facing an enemy none of us understand.

Amber finally married a Mormon. It seemed to be her goal. We do love Brad, though.

Brad will be joining my long list of one other son in law, Jessye. Audrey met and married this awesome guy on the Fourth of July, 2003. They have Erica, Tryztyn and Xzaver.

Abbie stayed with my mother her Senior year so she could graduate from Bevier.

Allie had some emotional problems after she was hurt, and we are still dealing with that.

Anna, Austen and Angel are doing well.

Me? Well, after six years of chasing off every man I dated I finally gave up and decided I would stop trying. I taught Sunday school for eleven year olds, went on several missions, taught in churches about the dangers of Mormonism and other cults, and one day was asked out by my very own chiropractor!

"Is he kidding?" I thought. But I went out to a Cardinal's

148

game with him in St. Louis and absolutely fell in love! Dr. James B. Jorgenson and I were married yesterday!

October 8, 2010-

To him that overcometh
will I grant to sit with me in my throne,
Even as I also overcame,
And am set down with my Father in His throne.
--Revelation 3:21

We ended up at a place called Lucky Oyster for Adam's birthday party. Again, Charlotte had his pictures set up in a corner of the room. I'm not sure if the management realized just how large this party would grow before the night was over. Adam's friends and SEAL brothers just kept arriving.

Matt was able to come to the party, too. He brought his beautiful wife. They are such an awesome couple. He will be going to Afghanistan himself soon.

The food was great. It was funny when my Andy ordered a plate full of oysters and ate the whole thing. Then someone else sat at our table and asked the waitress what she recommended.

"Well, I don't recommend the oysters!" she said in all sincerity.

We all looked at Andy, as he was chewing up his last mouthful of the stuff. He just froze with a look of disgust on his face.

Somehow we all burst out laughing at poor Andy. Even though the waitress tried to explain that what she meant was that these particular oysters were shipped from the west coast. They usually got them from the east coast and there really wasn't anything wrong with them. Andy still downed his entire glass of water in one sitting.

It felt bitter sweet to actually have a moment of laughter there with my children, knowing we would be forever sad inside.

Around eight o clock the singer named Jack Becker was set up and ready to sing. Eric went over to him and told him the purpose of our party. He told him what happened to Adam and how much Adam enjoyed listening to him sing.

He told him that this was Adam's birthday party.

Mr. Becker introduced himself and then made an announcement.

"I'd like us all to sing Happy Birthday to a very special person, Adam Olin Smith."

Suddenly, a half intoxicated man who stood near me, who must have met Adam somewhere, lifted his glass and said, "Adam's here? Where is he?" Guess he hadn't heard.

Mr. Becker went on, "Adam lost his life in Afghanistan a couple weeks ago."

There was a moment of silence, then Jack Becker began to play Happy Birthday. Everyone sang and most of us cried. It was the most beautiful sound of love and pain I've ever experienced.

Immediately, Jack went into the song, 'I'm Proud to be an American.' Everyone stood and joined in singing as loud as they could.

As always, I was proud to be an American.

August 18 , 2007-

He that overcometh,
the same shall be clothed in white raiment;
And I will not blot out his name out of the book of life,
But I will confess his name before my Father,
and before His angels.
--Revelation 3:5

My Adam has finally graduated from BUDS! It seemed like it would never happen. He stuck with it though. Two weeks after he suffered from the man-made pneumonia, he called me.

"Mom, my right side is really hurting." This was coming from one of my children who rarely complained of any health problems.

"Let me ask you this, can you swim today with it?"

"I can't even stand up straight."

"Well, I'm no doctor. At first I thought it may be left over pain from your pneumonia, but now It sounds a lot like it's your appendix. You should probably get it checked out."

150

"I can't do that Mom. They don't like it if we go to the hospital here. I'm already rolled back to the next class. I think they will definitely kick me out if I have another medical problem."

"You need to tell them now, or I will fly out there and tell them myself."

Adam's appendix had ruptured. That night he went to surgery. But, for some strange reason, they did not kick him out of Navy SEAL training.

He endured to the end!

October 8, 2010-

And behold, I come quickly; and my reward is with me,
to give to every man according as his work shall be.
I am Alpha and Omega, the beginning and the end,
the first and the last.
--Revelation 22:12-13

The party for Adam's 27th birthday continued for hours. As is the Navy tradition, there was much drinking. I tried to mingle, but the place was so crowded. I stood for quite some time and spoke with a young widow. I had met several young widows who had lost their spouses to this war. We connected and had a great conversation about life and death.

Charlotte had a huge cake made for Adam. Although I usually don't like cake, I wanted her to smile, so I accepted a piece.

In time, I became uncomfortable at the party. I'm not a heavy drinker, so I used the excuse that I was tired to go back to Adam's house. It worked. Amber, who isn't supposed to drink even caffeine, wanted to leave, too.

We caught a ride with Adam's Scottish neighbors. They were hilarious. All the way back they told these unbelievable stories about themselves and their lives.

"Once when my husband was driving us home," she told in her native accent, "he was driving so fast and reckless that I told him 'do you actually want to make a vegetable of me?' He was quiet for a moment and then said to me, 'if you could be a vegetable, which one would you like to

be?'"

I'm not sure how funny the story was but just to hear the two of them go on with each other was delightful.

At last we arrived at Adam's.

I worked on packing my things and looking through Adam's boxes. I found many of the pictures I had sent him through the years of the children growing up. I found my letters to him and cried as I read them.

There was an Army green helmet with his last name inside. I thought of the times he had played "soldier" as a child. My heart started hurting, and I felt like I could choke.

I went downstairs and fell asleep on the couch wrapped in the brown afghan I had crocheted for him.

September 2, 2010-

Behold I come quickly:
Blessed is he that keepeth the sayings
of the prophesy of this Book.
--Revelation 22:7

My Adam has been home for a visit. It has been the best time ever since he enlisted! Usually when he comes home I may get twenty minutes to an hour of his time. Sometimes some of the children don't get to see him at all.

Not this time! We have all enjoyed him so much. He went to the Bevier Homecoming a couple weeks ago and then that Saturday he attended the Smith family reunion.

That afternoon he came to my house. He and the other children were all fired up and rowdy. I was just glad to have most of them at home at the same time.

We were all in the living room when suddenly Adam said, "Hey, I know, let's play charades!"

We all became very quiet and just looked at him as if he would start laughing or something to let us know he was just joking.

"No, I'm serious. Let's play it. Here I've got the game downloaded into my phone."

We knew he meant it, and we all just laughed to see this big tough Navy SEAL standing there with charades on his phone. We played that game together and laughed so hard our sides hurt to see Adam get so involved in it.

I watched my son that day and was so very pleased at how he had changed. He had a glow about him and was truly the happiest I had seen him since he was a little boy. I wondered what exactly made him that way. Could it be his girlfriend, Charlotte? Could it be the Navy SEALs? Could it be that he had finally realized that the Lord was with him and he felt safe? Or was it a combination of it all?

Whatever it was, the other children and I were just drawn to his handsome smiling face.

"Hey, you guys have to promise me that you will get together here tomorrow and take a picture of you all," I pleaded with them later that day as they began to say they had to leave. "You know how I am about pictures."

They promised they would meet, even though I had to help with an open house for the pregnancy center the next day. I felt a pang of regret to miss an opportunity to be with all my babies at the same time, but knew there would be other times in the future.

I heard stories of how they all decided it would look more mysterious if they took the pictures on the nearby rail road tracks. My James and Brad went along to actually snap the pictures.

Adam returned to Virginia.

Today, I was driving home from Columbia when I just felt very strongly I needed to talk to him. Usually I call him later at night, but I just went ahead and rang his number. He answered right away.

"Mom, what's up?"

"Nothing, Bud, just wondered what you are doing."

"I'm packing."

"Where are you going?"

"Mom, I leave tomorrow for Afghanistan."

"What!"

"I told you, didn't I?"

"I think I would remember that bit of information!"

"Sorry, Mom, I told everyone else, I thought I told you too."

"It's OK, Bud, this is big. I will be praying for you every day."

"Thanks, Mom."

"I love you, Adam."

"I love you too, Mom. Goodbye."

153

October 9, 2010-

And the Spirit and the bride say, Come.
And let him that heareth say, Come.
And let him that is athirst come.
And whosoever will, let him take the water of life freely.
--Revelation 22:17

Sometime in the early morning hours, I heard the others who were staying at Adam's house return. Quietly, I hurried up to his room and fell back asleep.

Sunlight was peeking through the window when I awoke. It was early. Most of the others would not be up for hours. I got up and dressed and straightened up Adam's bed. I hated to leave the last place my son lived.

Once downstairs I tip toed past sleeping people to the back door. The two dogs that belong to Josh's girlfriend were right there waiting for someone to open the door. We all went outside.

Sitting on the bench swing by the fence, I watched the animals play. I tried to keep from crying as I wondered how long ago my son had sat in this same seat. How many good times had he spent out here entertaining his friends and Charlotte?

Speaking of Charlotte, I could see her looking out the window. She must have had a rough time sleeping last night, if she slept at all. I decided to go inside and spend some time with her.

We sat in the kitchen and made small talk, but I noticed she was unusually quiet and subdued. I wondered if it was the late night or all the events that had gone on for the past few weeks.

"I don't want you guys to leave," she finally said in a low voice with her bottom lip quivering.

"I know," was all I could think to say. "I wish you could come home with us."

Amber came in then, and our conversation turned to travel talk. Charlotte slipped back into her role of hostess.

It seemed like no time at all when we were walking towards the door to leave. I hugged Charlotte close and cried.

"Can you have the afghan I made for Adam cleaned, and

154

then give it to Little Wally's new baby nephew?" It was a strange request for me to make, but it was a very masculine colored cover and I wanted the baby to have something from Adam. He would have been around to watch this young man grow up I'm sure.

"Yes, I will," Charlotte assured me.

We hugged again, then told her how grateful we were that Adam had found her, even though their time together had been cut short.

As we were driven to the airport, I looked back one last time at the only house my son would own. I knew I would never see it again.

We caravanned the short distance to the airport. Matt came along on his motorcycle to say goodbye. I rode with his wife and two adorable children. When I hugged him I felt as if I were saying goodbye to one of my own children. He teared up, too.

"If you need anything, you can call me," he told me sadly.

"I will. Thank you so much for all you've done for my family. I know we would not have made it through this without your help."

He stood there on the sidewalk as we entered the airport.

For the next hour we were kept busy with our luggage and tickets and boarding the flight home.

For some reason, I was seated in the back of the plane and the rest of my children were towards the front. It was fine with me, as I needed time to ponder the last few weeks of my life.

"What just happened?" I asked myself. "Is it true and possible that I just lost one of my children?"

This time I was ready with tissues, and just let the tears flow. No one was sitting next to me or seemed to be paying attention to me.

All the events were over. There was nothing left on my calendar to attend. Nothing faced me at home that had to do with my son.

"Father, this cannot be the end of my Adam Olin! An entire life cannot just be wrapped up and put away in three simple weeks! He will be forgotten!"

"Then write a book."

"Write a book? I will! I will tell everyone the story of

Adam. And You will be in it too, Father! I will tell how You have never left us, even in our darkest hour, especially in our darkest hour!

"It will be a book about hope!"

The Beginning

EPILOGUE

For thou art my hope, o Lord God:
Thou art my trust from my youth.
--Psalm 71:5

August 1, 2011-
Osama bin Laden has been killed in Pakistan by our very own United States Navy SEALs! Some say I should not be happy at the death of anyone. I say, "Shout praises to the heavens above!"

How is my family doing today?

Amber Marie will be giving birth to my twelfth grandchild near Thanksgiving this year.

Audrey Loraine is signing up for EMT classes.

Andrew Lee continues to serve in the Missouri National Guard.

Abigail Rose delivered our baby Olin on Christmas Day of 2010.

Alaina Grace works several jobs and is raising precious Jericho.

Anna Kay graduated high school and seeks a career in Child Development.

Austen Edward, my football player, has come to know the Lord and wants to help others.

Angel Rae loves basketball and wants to be a pediatrician someday.

James remains a rock to our family.

Although time moves on, children grow up, and life continues, there seems to be a part of me that lies broken on some distant mountainside in Afghanistan.

Yet, there is a flicker of hope which will always burn within me. My Adam's life was a vapor but his spirit lives on. He may be watching me even now. Someday I will be reunited with him in heaven, and he will say, "Mom, Mom, Mom, there's SOMEONE I want you to meet!"

Author Michele Jorgenson

Michele Jorgenson, author of _FROM HELL WEEK TO HEAVEN: The Life and Times of Adam Olin Smith,_ is a founder of Ray of Hope Pregnancy Care Ministries. She is a cult survivor and active in assisting others who may have been deceived.

Jorgenson is active in Christian missions both inside and outside of the United States. She has taught in Sunday schools and Bible Schools, coached basketball and soccer at the YMCA, is a substitute teacher and works as an EMT.

Currently residing in Macon, Missouri with her husband, James and the youngest three of her nine children, Jorgenson has been blessed to have been the mother of Adam Olin Smith, and eagerly awaits the second coming of our Lord, Jesus Christ so that they can once again be united.